HENRY DAVID THOREAU

A CRITICAL STUDY

HENRY DAVID THOREAU

A CRITICAL STUDY

BY

MARK VAN DOREN

New York

RUSSELL & RUSSELL

1961

TO

MY FATHER AND MOTHER

PREFACE

THIS study is founded pretty largely, it will be seen, on Thoreau's Journal, which has not been examined before, so far as I know, with much attention to chronology. If new emphasis has been placed here or there, it is because new ground has been covered. If now and then unwelcome conclusions are arrived at, the Journal is to blame; the Journal is important, I think, not because it is the most attractive, but because it is the most complete, picture of Thoreau's mind.

I am led to attach a preface to so slight an essay mainly by the consciousness of certain debts which I have incurred while occupied with Thoreau, and which I desire very much to acknowledge somewhere. The essay owes most to Professor S. P. Sherman, of the University of Illinois, who was its constant stimulus when it was being written, and to my brother, Carl Van Doren, who gave invaluable aid when it was being revised. Professor A. H. Thorndike and Professor W. P. Trent, of Columbia University, kindly read the manuscript, and made important suggestions. Mr. George S. Hellman generously

gave me *carte blanche* with his Thoreau posses-
sions. Mr. F. H. Allen brought his accurate
knowledge of Thoreau to bear upon the essay as
it was going through the press.

M. V. D.

CONTENTS

HENRY DAVID THOREAU

I

THE SOLITARY

The character and the works of Henry David Thoreau, who chose to live alone in the world, have roused stabbing assailants like Lowell and Stevenson, or complete panegyrists like Emerson and the biographers, but few critics. In the twentieth century it is desirable not so much to condemn or justify the whole of Thoreau as to describe and explain his parts, not so much to take or reject the whole of his shrewdly propounded doctrine as to decide wherein only and wherein not at all his extraordinary and undoubted spiritual value lies; and now, when virtually all he wrote is in print, such a study becomes possible. It becomes possible both to ask the reason for his living to himself — how much it was his nature, how much it was his theory; and to ask the consequences of the life he lived — how valuable his theory, how important his personality? If in the present essay the ends of his thinking seem to be sought exclusively in the Journal, the excuse is that only in the Journal did Thoreau think to the end; it was his misfortune that to think to the end transcendentally was to think extravagantly; it is nowhere pretended that this is his most important thinking; it is never forgotten that the best of him is not the raw Journal.

Thoreau states his theory of solitude as clearly as relentlessly. Whoever is solitary by nature, says Aristotle, is either a wild beast or a god. Thoreau hints now and then that he feels himself in the company of gods; certainly his approach to the arcanum of solitude betrays the morning worshiper. The slender musing of William Drummond in Hawthornden; the jaunty salute of Cotton and Walton,

> " Farewell, thou busy world, and may
> We never meet again ";

the gentlemanly retreat of Cowley; the Horatian pose of Pope; the hermitage of the eighteenth-century sentimentalist; the plaintive self-assurance of Shelley, "a nightingale who sits in darkness and sings to cheer its own solitude with sweet sounds"; the mellow confidence of Wordsworth in his mountain surroundings; the pugnacity of Landor, who strove with none; the quizzical fancy of Hazlitt for "living to one's self"; the terrible nakedness of Carlyle at twenty-three, "wandering over the moors like a restless spirit"; the mock bravery of Browning, hoisting his soul amid infinite din, — none of these has either the quiet consecrated relentlessness of Thoreau's passion or the salt of his irony. Nor does the sense of futility that is in the youthful Arnold haunt Thoreau as it haunted most men of letters in the nineteenth century; Thoreau never shrank publicly from his metaphysics.

In America the long tradition of Puritan and Quaker inward awe, the exalted security of Bryant, and the lonely forests of Cooper take us but a little way toward Thoreau. Even within — the transcendental circle we find him apart. — Emerson, whose " strength and doom " was " to be solitary," and who set the fashion of solitude, anticipated the whole gist of Lowell's " Thoreau " when he reminded himself that " it is not the solitude of place, but the solitude of soul which is so estimable to us." Hawthorne, who did not conceal his personal horror of the spiritual vacuums he created in fiction, and Herman Melville, who shuddered throughout his " Moby Dick " to find his imagination " encompassed by all the horrors of the half-known life," — these clearly have not the self-sufficiency of Thoreau, of whom Emerson said, " He was bred to no profession; he never married; he lived alone; he never went to church; he never voted; he refused to pay a tax to the State; he ate no flesh,

he drank no wine, he never knew the use of to-
bacco; and, though a naturalist, he used neither
trap nor gun." Only Thoreau among the transcendentalists by constitution demanded lifelong
letting alone — was content (at least in theory)
with pure loneliness. Only Thoreau can be vis-
ualized as an isolated personality, lying prone on
the ice to explore the bottom of Walden Pond,
or reading Homer in his hut on bad nights, or
hoeing beans in quiet clearings, or strolling in
condescension towards the village, or talking to
a friend across the pond, or holding the world at
bay with a paradox.

Such is the Thoreau of " Walden " and the
" Week." But there is a wide space between
the public and the private Thoreau. The private
Thoreau was not all self-sufficiency. Speaking
always very stoutly, claiming to have been born
for solitude, and professing to find it " wholesome to be alone the greater part of the time,"
he still had not at center one third of the poise
and complacency of Emerson. What students
of Thoreau might always have suspected, the
fourteen volumes of his " Journal," betraying
the self-doubter in almost equal proportions with
the self-exploiter, now confirm.

Among the critics, the personality of Thoreau
has never been presented in full, mainly because
it has been treated in no case by any one who

was not interested in proving a point — that Thoreau was a hermit, that Thoreau was not a hermit, that Thoreau had pity and humor, that Thoreau was cold and inhuman, that Thoreau was a perfect stoic, that Thoreau was a sentimentalist, that Thoreau was a skulker. Emerson, who knew him best, cannot always be relied on to give a fair account of the man, because Emerson's interest in him was the interest of a philosophic father in a philosophic son; he spoke of him as "my Henry Thoreau"; he commended Thoreau the naturalist only because he practiced (or so Emerson believed) what Emerson the philosopher of Nature preached; and after Thoreau's death he edited a volume of letters which he said he had selected to represent "a perfect piece of stoicism." Thoreau had not bid for such an interpretation, or indeed for any interpretation. "You may rely on it that you have the best of me in my books, and that I am not worth seeing personally," he wrote to a friend in February, 1856. But it may be remembered that he hated visitors, and that if the best of him is in the books he published, by no means all of him is or can be there.

One is never in doubt that Thoreau's personality was not neutral, but pungent. Emerson found him too withdrawing in his later years; but Thoreau then believed that Emerson was

patronizing him,[1] and he certainly was no man
to bask for long at a time in the sun of Emersonian geniality. To a cool observer Thoreau
must have been most interesting for what has
been called the "fine aroma" of his character.
At least his personality was positive enough to
hold its own with the other transcendentalists.
Stevenson took the cue for his remarkable criticism of Thoreau's disposition from the "thin,
penetrating, big-nosed face." The face, even the
whole figure, is significant. The Rowse crayon [2]
and the Worcester daguerreotype [3] both show
a face by no means simple to describe — con-
temptuous yet sensitive, aglint with irony yet
dissolved in the pains of self, cold yet sensuous,
alert yet lonely. His figure was unusually slight,
with sloping shoulders and narrow chest, but it
was "alive with Thoreau." Emerson's statement
that there was "somewhat military in his nature" scarcely does justice to the quality of this
"life" in Thoreau's body. There was much of
determination; his hand was habitually clenched;
in walking he was a "noticeable man," with "his
eyes bent on the ground, his long swinging gait,
his hands perhaps clasped behind him, or held

[1] Thoreau's *Journal*, III, 256. The references hereafter to
Thoreau's works are to the volumes of the Walden Edition, 20
vols., Boston: Houghton Mifflin Company, 1906.

[2] 1854. Frontispiece of vol. I of the *Journal*.

[3] 1856. Frontispiece of the *Week*.

closely at his side." There was also much of
wildness; Hawthorne thought him something of
an Indian, found him " wild, original — as ugly
as sin," with uncouth though courteous manners.
Alcott was "touched by his aboriginal vigor,"
and a younger observer jotted down these notes
in his diary after his first sight of Thoreau:
" Thoreau looks eminently *sagacious* — like a
sort of wise, wild beast . . . a ruddy weather-
beaten face, which reminds me of some shrewd
and honest animal's — some retired philosophical
woodchuck or magnanimous fox. . . . He walks
about with a brisk, rustic air, and never seems
tired."

Thoreau's ancestry reveals very few secrets.
His racial inheritance is as interesting as it is
complicated ; but it is too simple to conjecture,
as writers have done, that he derived his narrow-
ness from the Scotch, his tendency to hold an
extreme logical position from the French, his
wistfulness and his wildness from the Celts, his
clear, pure mysticism from the Quakers, or his
sense of moral responsibility from the Puritans.
It would be more reasonable to inquire what his
immediate family must have meant to him. There
is little to be known, and less that is significant,
even here. The father, it seems, gave Thoreau
scarcely more than his workmanlike quality ; we
hear that he was "a cautious man, a close ob-

server, methodical and deliberate in action," who
"produced excellent results." The mother con-
tributed, it is to be supposed, quick wit, high
spirits, audacity, and alertness.

Those qualities of Thoreau's mind and heart
which a wise reader will not forget are six : sensibility, concreteness of vision, thoroughness,
wild combative self-sufficiency, humor, and wistfulness.

Thoreau was more at the mercy of his senses
than a perfect piece of stoicism is expected to
be. "He had many elegances of his own," says
Emerson. "Thus, he could not bear to hear the
sound of his own steps, the grit of gravel ; and
therefore never willingly walked in the road,
but in the grass, on mountains and in woods."
The sight of a suffering fugitive slave could strike
extraordinary pity from him. One of the most
effective chapters in " Walden" is on "Sounds,"
and his passion for music was more than philosophical — sometimes almost " tore him to
pieces." He betrays a sensitiveness in his human relationships which one is tempted to em-
ploy for explaining his very aloofness. He could
not speak of his brother John Thoreau's death,
twelve years after it had occurred, "without
physical suffering, so that when he related it to
his friend Ricketson at New Bedford, he turned
pale and was forced to go to the door for air."

Certainly he was not at center the iron-cold structure of Stevenson's essay. Indeed, it is possible that his indifference was after all only a superstructure built on a very unfirm foundation, that his whole "stoic" career was the career of one who demanded desperately the right to feel what he pleased as secretly but as powerfully as he pleased. This story is told of Thoreau at nineteen or twenty: " While in college he once asked his mother what profession she would have him choose. She said, pleasantly, 'You can buckle on your knapsack, dear, and roam abroad to seek your fortune'; but the thought of leaving home and forsaking Concord made the tears roll down his cheeks. Then his sister Helen, who was standing by, tenderly put her arm around him and kissed him, saying, 'No, Henry, you shall not go; you shall stay at home and live with us.' " That youth was not the Cato he is supposed by many to have been. He preferred Concord to cosmopolitanism for a reason. He cannot reprove the world for having emotions.

If Thoreau felt and saw and heard much, he also felt and saw and heard concretely. In his writing and in his living his genius for the specific, his preoccupation with details, his love of facts, and his passion for real experience mark him off as distinctly as is possible from his transcendental brethren. His handiness with tools, which the pencil-making evinces, has become almost proverbial. He seemed eminently sensible to his friends; Hawthorne found in him "a basis of good sense" and thought him "a healthy and wholesome man to know." Alcott knowingly refers to his "russet probity and good sense." Certainly an utter sincerity and a passion for genuine experience were in him. "There are nowadays professors of philosophy, but not philosophers," he writes in "Walden." "To be a philosopher is not merely to have subtle thoughts, nor even to found a school, but so to love wisdom as to live according to its dictates, a life of simplicity, independence, magnanimity, and trust."

What Emerson preached in smiling benignity, his disciple Thoreau lived and described with amazing thoroughness, with set lips. He kept both his poise and his singleness of aim intact; he was always on tiptoe ready for a new experience; he could pursue a subject of conversation more relentlessly and longer than could any other in the company. Even if he were insignificant in that he took all of his ideas from Emerson, he would still be significant in that he reduced them to their practicable and visualizable essence.

He not only suited himself in solitude, but went out and challenged more social souls to combat. Even as early as one of his college essays, he attacked "the man of the world" as a "viper." Living "extempore," living the life of whim that Emerson recommended, Thoreau was unpleasant to contradict, and dangerous to curb. He had none of what he called "a false shame lest he be considered singular and eccentric." He lived by instinct on the defensive, striking back constantly with paradox, and steadily throwing up works around his person and his philosophy with assertion. "Thoreau is with difficulty sweet," said Emerson. Thoreau rarely bothered about being sweet. He had an appetite for sarcasm and a gift for rejoinder, and often indulged both purely for his own satisfaction in closed pages of the Journal. He was a voluble talker, and did not spare his fellow townsmen any criticism. Stevenson most absurdly charges him with a "hatred of a genuine brand, hot as Corsican revenge, and sneering like Voltaire." Emerson's gentler judgment, that "he did not feel himself except in opposition," comes much closer to the truth.

Thoreau had more of native humor than any of the transcendentalists, just as he had a livelier appreciation of facts. If "Walden" is the best transcendental book, that is partly because it was written in bounding spirits, with eyes twinkling and tongue in cheek. Cynical generally, satur-

nine, impish on occasions, always pointed, his
humor sometimes broadened into boisterousness.
When Ellery Channing visited Thoreau at Walden, the two "made that small house ring with
boisterous mirth." There are puns in the Letters
and the Journal which only pure fun could order.
There is testimony that Thoreau liked to come
down from his study of evenings to dance or
whistle or sing; and he sang "Tom Bowline"
with considerable relish. He had scarcely the
"cast-iron quaintness" which Dickens observed
in the New England transcendentalists, but he
had another New England trait : he saw pretty
far at times into human nature, and found his
humor there. It was his saving humor, finally,
which trimmed the excesses of his Journal when
he went into print.

Throughout all Thoreau's professions of self-
sufficiency sound hauntings of dissatisfaction
and wistfulness, which, Celtic or not, are by no
means the equivalent of the indefinite yearning
of the German romanticists, but give hint of a
very real passion in Thoreau's make-up. There are
traces of pure affection now and then which
Stevenson was blind to. He was guide and
teacher for children on berrying parties. There
are youthful love poems to be accounted for, and
rumors of a love-affair. And there is the famous
paragraph in "Walden," by no means clear on the

face of it, and not yet explained, which Emerson calls "the mythical record of his disappointments" : —

"I long ago lost a hound, a bay horse, and a turtle-dove, and am still on their trail. Many are the travellers I have spoken concerning them, describing their tracks and what calls they answered to. I have met one or two who had heard the hound, and the tramp of the horse, and even seen the dove disappear behind a cloud, and they seemed as anxious to recover them as if they had lost them themselves."

So much of personal wistfulness, most of it never expressed, in this passage veiled by allegory, suggests that there was something with which Thoreau was not completely satisfied, and that this was neither the transcendental universe nor the will-o'-the-wisps of Beauty and the Present, but some one of the human relationships themselves.

II

FRIENDSHIP ; NATURE

rooster

"SURELY joy is the condition of life," wrote this chanticleer of the nineteenth century. It is perfectly obvious that he would have his readers shun melancholy as they would shun the Devil. He, at least in his capacity of author and lecturer, will be no moping owl to complain that existence is desperate. He will not have it that an author's life is hard — he to whom "to be hindered from accomplishing" his literary labors in the Walden hermitage (whither he went, as every one knows, to assemble the "Week" from several years of the Journal) "for want of a little common sense, a little enterprise and business talent, appeared not so sad as foolish." Tingling with idealism, exalted by freedom, like chanticleer on tiptoe quivering with expansion, Thoreau could veil his disappointments.[1]

[1] The title-page of the first edition of *Walden* (1854) bore this legend, printed beneath a captivating woodcut of Thoreau's Walden "hermitage," and repeated on page 92 of the ensuing text: "I do not propose to write an ode to dejection, but to brag as lustily as chanticleer in the morning, standing on his roost, if only to wake my neighbors up." The sentence signified more to Thoreau and his first readers than is generally realized. Some unpublished pages of Thoreau's Journal in the possession of Mr. George S. Hellman, of New York, are

But he did not blot the sadness he could veil.
" He had many reserves," says Emerson, " and

intensely interesting as containing two quotations jotted down
by Thoreau without ascription or comment as if in a common-
place-book, one of which is from Coleridge's *Ode to Dejection:*

> " It were a vain endeavor,
>   Though I should gaze forever
> On that green light that lingers in the west:
> I may not hope from outward forms to win
> The passion and the life, whose fountains are within.
> . . . .
> I see them all so excellently fair,
> I see, not feel, how beautiful they are !
> . . . .
> O Lady ! We receive but what we give,
> And in our life alone does Nature live."

At the end of the passage Thoreau interposes, " And thus
sounds another's wail," and goes on to quote from Byron's
Don Juan:

> " No more — no more — Oh! never more on me
>   The freshness of the heart can fall like dew,
> Which out of all the lovely things we see
>   Extracts emotions beautiful and new,
> Hived in our bosoms like the bag o' the bee :
>   Think'st thou the honey with these objects grew ?
> Alas ! 't was not in them, but in thy power
> To double even the sweetness of a flower.

> " No more — no more — Oh! never more, my heart,
>   Canst thou be my sole world, my universe !
> Once all in all, but now a thing apart,
>   Thou canst not be my blessing or my curse :
> The illusion 's gone forever."

The pages on which these lines are entered are undated, but
it is safe to assume that they belong among the first pages of
the Journal, since Thoreau did most of his quoting early. The
two quotations, and more particularly the tone of the remark
written between them, are important as showing Thoreau setting his face early and definitely against the winds of philosophic despair that blew throughout the nineteenth century.
The lines from Coleridge and Byron were, of course, widely
known and felt in those days. The lines from Coleridge ex-

knew how to throw a poetic veil over his experience." He threw no poetic veil over his Journal,
which was his experience ; and he left elsewhere
a litter which is easy to collect and with the testimony of which it is easy to indict him on the
charge of experiencing disillusionment.

The parable of the hound, the bay horse, and
the turtle-dove is plainly a "mythical record of
disappointments." But what disappointments has
been a question. What his quest was he never
told ; not that he was ignorant himself, not that
it was anything like the blue flower of Novalis,
a symbol of indefinite and infinite yearning ; but
" he had many reserves." His quest was the
present, the self, the secret of Nature, or Real-

actly expressed John Stuart Mill's youthful pessimism, Mill confesses in the *Autobiography*. When Tennyson went in 1848 to
visit the Reverend Stephen Hawker, the latter observed : " His
temper seemed very calm. His spirits very low. When I quoted,
' O never more on me,' etc., he said they too were his haunting
words." That Thoreau was not only crowing to keep up his
own courage, but was willing to crow against the storm for all
mankind, is attested by his pen-sketch of chanticleer on the
manuscript title-page which he drew up originally for *Walden*
and which has been reproduced in the edition of *Walden* published by the Bibliophile Society of Boston. Under the chanticleer legend on the same page is a quotation from Sadi (never
printed), which offers Thoreau's solution of the whole problem
of living — implicit obedience to Nature : " The clouds, wind,
moon, sun and sky act in coöperation that thou mayest get thy
daily bread, and not eat it with indifference ; all revolve for
thy sake, and are obedient to command ; it must be an equi-
table condition, that thou shalt be obedient also."

ity, say his commentators ; and if Thoreau were
entirely unknown personally, any of these con-
jectures might be plausible. Thus if one were
setting out to prove the case for " the present,"
one would find Thoreau reminding himself that
he " must live above all in the present ";[1] and
declaring in 1850[2] "In all my travels I never
came to the abode of the present." But it is clear
enough that Thoreau's quest was not for any
metaphysical entity, because he wore his metaphysics as comfortably as any one. It is clear
enough that this single disappointment of his
life was not an intellectual but an emotional one,
and that it arose in the domain of the human relations. His ideal was perfection in human intercourse, and his quest was for an absolutely satisfactory condition of friendship.

The evidence is the Journal and a passage in
the " Dial." In March of 1842,[3] Thoreau wrote,
" Where is my heart gone? They say men cannot part with it and live." A year later he edited
for the " Dial "[4] passages from the " Chinese Four
Books," one paragraph of which, astonishing for
its resemblances to the famous parable, reads thus :
" Benevolence is man's heart, and justice is man's
path. If a man lose his fowls or his dogs, he knows
how to seek them. There are those who lose their

[1] *Journal*, II, 138.   [2] *Ibid.*, II, 74.
[3] *Ibid.*, I, 350.   [4] *Dial*, IV, 206.

hearts and know not how to seek them. The duty of the student is no other than to seek his lost heart." There is good reason to believe that Thoreau, putting his own construction upon this passage, employed it eleven years later in " Walden " to veil a personal longing which was genuine and keen and which demanded expression if only through parable. A year before " Walden " appeared, he was writing:[1] " No fields are so barren to me as the men of whom I expect everything but get nothing. In their neighborhood I experience a painful yearning for society, which cannot be satisfied."

What was Thoreau's hope from abstract friendship, and where are the unmistakable signs of his disappointment?

No one ever spoke more loftily about friendship. " No one else, to my knowledge," says Stevenson, " has spoken in so high and just a spirit of the kindly relations ; and I doubt whether it be a drawback that these lessons should come from one in many ways so unfitted to be a teacher in this branch. . . . The very coldness and egoism of his intercourse gave him a clearer insight into the intellectual basis of our warm, mutual tolerations." No one ever claimed more for friendship. " All those contingencies," wrote Thoreau in 1841,[2] " which the philanthropist, statesman, and house-

[1] *Journal*, v, 87.   [2] *Ibid.*, i, 190.

keeper write so many books to meet are simply and quietly settled in the intercourse of friends." No one ever expected more from friendship. In 1843 he wrote to a friend, "We always seem to be living just on the brink of a pure and lofty intercourse which would make the ills and trivialness of life ridiculous. After each little interval, though it be but for the night, we are prepared to meet each other as gods and goddesses."

At the same time, no one was ever more disappointed in friendship. Thoreau speaks his disappointment in two voices. One voice is for the world which he has found inadequate, has the tone of sharp reproof and the manner of the cynic philosopher, and expresses contempt for "that old musty cheese that we are." "In what concerns you much," he wrote, "do not think that you have companions; know that you are alone in the world." "How alone must our life be lived! We dwell on the seashore, and none between us and the sea. Men are my merry companions, my fellow-pilgrims, who beguile the way but leave me at the first turn of the road, for none are travelling one road so far as myself." It was in this key that his acquaintances found him strung; it was the man "who never felt himself except in opposition" that Emerson is complaining of here in his Journal: [1] "If I knew only Thoreau, I should think coöper-

---

[1] Emerson's *Journal*, ix, 15.

ation of good men impossible. Must we always talk for victory, and never once for truth, for comfort, and joy? Centrality he has and penetration, strong understanding, and the higher gifts — but all this and all his resources of wit and invention are lost to me in every experiment, year after year, that I make, to hold intercourse with his mind. Always some weary, captious paradox to fight you with, and the time and temper wasted." Thoreau is found reporting from his side a conversation with Emerson:[1] "P. M. — Talked, or tried to talk, with R. W. E. Lost my time — nay, almost my identity. He, assuming a false opposition where there was no difference of opinion, talked to the wind — told me what I knew — and I lost my time trying to imagine myself somebody else to oppose him." It is plain that very little can be learned about Thoreau's private feeling in the matter of friendship from his published writings or from his conversations; in what he published he scowled and strutted; in conversation he rose up like a gamecock at flutter of opposition and never lowered his head. Emerson and Thoreau are peers in egoism; they tell nothing about each other.

Thoreau's other voice is for himself; its very persistence distinguishes him from his transcendental fellows. "Love is a thirst that is never

[1] *Journal*, v, 188.

slaked," he wrote in his Journal.[1] No one outside knew what was needed to quench that thirst,
precisely because no one could even be sure of
its existence. "You are not living altogether as
I could wish," wrote Thomas Cholmondeley, an
English friend, to Thoreau in 1856. "You ought
to have society. A college, a conventual life is for
you. You should be the member of some society
not yet formed. . . . Without this you will be
liable to moulder away as you get older. Your
love for Nature is ancillary to some affection
which you have not yet discovered. The great
Kant never dined alone. Once, when there was
a danger of the empty dinner table, he sent his
valet out, bidding him catch the first man he
could find and bring him in! So necessary was
the tonic, the effervescing cup of conversation, to
his deeper labors. . . . The lonely man is a dis-
eased man, I greatly fear. See how carefully Mr.
Emerson avoids it; and yet, who dwells, in all
essentials, more religiously free than he? . . .
By such a course you would not lose Nature.
But supposing that reasons, of which I can know
nothing, determine you to remain in 'quasi' retirement; still, let not this retirement be too lonely."
Thoreau did not need to be told all that, hoping
as he continually was in his solitude that the
quality of affection would be born, that the hound,

[1] *Journal*, VIII, 231.

the horse, and the turtle-dove would pause and wait for him and consent to be stroked.

The history of Thoreau's personal experiences in friendship is written in the early poems and in the Journal. They give one best to understand what were the nature and requirements of his ideal.

" His biography is in his verses," said Emerson. The poems serve best, perhaps, to prove both that his ideal of human intercourse was with him from the first, and that the personal, real affection for which he yearned was never the affection of or for this or that particular person, but was the sentiment of affection, or the capacity for affection, itself — that thing which, too late to mend matters, he found had been ruled, perhaps without his consent, out of his life. There were rumors of an unreturned, even martyred love, for one Ellen Sewall, and the lines from his first contribution to the " Dial," " Sympathy," —

" Each moment as we nearer drew to each,
   A stern respect withheld us farther yet,
So that we seemed beyond each other's reach,
   And less acquainted than when first we met," —

have been said to refer covertly to his relations with her. It is hinted darkly that "certain sonnets which he addressed to her will some day see the light." Many have sentimentalized the

legend. As a matter of fact, the evidence that
Thoreau ever loved any particular woman is ex-
ceedingly slight. To Mrs. Emerson in 1843 he
writes, " You must know that you represent to me
woman, for I have not traveled very far or wide."
Eyes trained from birth on infinity, uncompro-
mising always in friendship as in other matters,
it is unlikely that he regretted much the absence
of a living heart. It was his constitutional want
of so desirable and fundamental an organ — a
want only accentuated by his philosophy — that
perplexed and saddened him. The verses " To
the Maiden in the East" cannot be autobio-
graphical so much as expressive of the fastidious
ideal of love that Thoreau's youthful melancholy
had fashioned out of the egoistic materials of
his temperament. Its strenuous delicacy and
plaintive laboriousness are wholly characteristic
of Thoreau's early verse.

> " It was a summer eve,
>   The air did gently heave
>   While yet a low-hung cloud
>   Thy eastern skies did shroud ;
>   The lightning's silent gleam,
>   Startling my drowsy dream
>   Seemed like the flash
>   Under thy dark eyelash.
>
>   .   .   .   .   .   .
>
> " Direct thy pensive eye
>   Into the western sky ;

And when the evening star
Does glimmer from afar
Upon the mountain line,
Accept it for a sign
  That I am near,
And thinking of thee here.

.   .   .   .   .   .

" I 'll walk with gentle pace,
And choose the smoothest place,
And careful dip the oar,
And shun the winding shore,
And gently steer my boat
Where water-lilies float,
  And cardinal-flowers
Stand in their sylvan bowers."

Some lines of the same period, —

" My love must be as free
As is the eagle's wing,"

and

" Let such pure hate still underprop
Our love, that we may be
Each other's conscience,"

with their blither, cooler notes, confirm the judgment that Thoreau was only idealizing from the beginning.

The Journal, containing a wealth of self-revelation of a character which a reader only of Thoreau's books does not dream of, continues the history of Thoreau's experiences in friendship. "My Journal should be the record of my love," writes Thoreau in the second volume.[1]

[1] *Journal*, II, 101.

In 1845 he first struck fire in friction with society, when he was arrested for refusing to pay taxes; and lost a friend or two. Henceforth his path is by no means a smooth one; doubts much more substantial than the yearning he could veil with allegory assail him. A series of extracts from the Journal (or elsewhere) can, better than anything else, indicate the real qualities of Thoreau's temper and the trend of his feeling for friends and for mankind.

1850:[1] " I love my friends very much, but I find that it is of no use to go to see them. I hate them commonly when I am near them."

1850:[2] " I go and see my friend and try his atmosphere. If our atmospheres do not mingle, if we repel each other strongly, it is of no use to stay."

1851:[3] " I wish my neighbors were wilder."

1851:[4] " What is the use of going to see people whom yet you never see, and who never see you? I begin to suspect that it is not necessary that we should see one another. . . . The society of young women is the most unprofitable I have ever tried. They are so light and flighty that you can never be sure whether they are there or not there. I prefer to talk with the more staid and settled, *settled for life*, in every sense."

[1] *Journal*, ii, 98. [2] *Ibid.*, ii, 109.
[3] *Ibid.*, ii, 171. [4] *Ibid.*, iii, 116.

1851:[1] "Ah, I yearn toward thee, my friend, but I have not confidence in thee. . . . I am not thou; thou art not I."

1851:[2] "It would give me such joy to know that a friend had come to see me, and yet that pleasure I seldom if ever experience."

1851:[3] " I seem to be more constantly merged in nature; my intellectual life is more obedient to nature than formerly, but perchance less obedient to spirit. I have less memorable seasons. I exact less of myself. . . . O if I could be discontented with myself! "

1852:[4] "If I have not succeeded in my friendships, it was because I demanded more of them and did not put up with what I could get; and I got no more partly because I gave so little."

1852:[5] "I go away to cherish my idea of friendship. Is not friendship a great relation?"

1856:[6] " And now another friendship is ended. I do not know what has made my friend doubt me, but I know that in love there is no mistake, and that every estrangement is well founded. But my destiny is not narrowed, but if possible the broader for it."

1856:[7] "Farewell, my friends. . . . For a long time you have appeared further and further

[1] *Journal*, III, 61.   [2] *Ibid.*, III, 150.
[3] *Ibid.*, III, 66.   [4] *Ibid.*, III, 262.
[5] *Ibid.*, IV, 314.   [6] *Ibid.*, IX, 249.
[7] *Ibid.*, VIII, 231.

off to me. I see that you will at length disappear altogether."

1857:[1] "If I should make the least concession, my friend would spurn me."

1857:[2] "I have tried them [men] ... they did not inspire me ... I lost my time. But out there [in Nature]! Who shall criticise that companion? It is like the hone to the knife. ... Shall I prefer a part, an infinitely small fraction, to the whole?"

1857:[3] "It does look sometimes as if the world were on its last legs. ... It would be sweet to deal with men more, I can imagine, but where dwell they? Not in the fields which I traverse."

1862:[4] "'The vine is dried up, and the fig tree languisheth; the pomegranate tree, the palm tree also, and the apple tree, even all the trees of the field, are withered; because joy is withered away from the sons of men.'"

"The meaning of Nature was never attempted to be defined by him," said Emerson. It is true that Thoreau did not dogmatize about Nature. Yet, time and again, in the Journal and elsewhere, he defined his own personal relation to her so clearly that no one now can mistake it. Such epithets as " companion," " club," " friend," and

---

[1] *Journal*, ix, 279. [2] *Ibid.*, ix, 216.
[3] *Ibid.*, ix, 205. [4] *Excursions*, "Wild Apples."

"bride" leave no uncertain impression. Nature
was Thoreau's best, because his only, friend.

Alcott considered that Thoreau had "the pro-
foundest passion for it [Nature] of any one living." Certainly there was no one like him in
America. The mere fact that he was a philosophic son of Emerson, who with the aid of Coleridge had joined Bacon with Plato, matter with
mind, nature with intellect, experiment with dialectic, sensation with ideas, to engender the transcendental Nature, does not furnish a reason or
an adequate motive for Thoreau's ruling passion.
Emerson, who indulged in "a breath under the
apple tree, a siesta on the grass, a whiff of
wind, an interval of retirement" only in order to
"revive the overtired brain" or in order to re-
store "the balance and serenity," understood that
Thoreau's bent was independent of his own influence, and declared that "his determination on
Natural History was organic." If Emerson studied Nature to know himself, Thoreau wedded
Nature to know himself.

"Remember thy Creator in the days of thy
Youth; i.e., lay up a store of natural influences,"
counseled Thoreau in 1851.[1] He never came
out from under those influences. As finely sus-
ceptible as Wordsworth, as passionate to report
his spiritual experiences, with a personality more

[1] *Journal*, II, 330.

pointed than Wordsworth's, he wore a rapt and
stealthy air in his approach to Nature which no
one else has shared. In the woods his face is said
to have shone with a light not seen in the village.
For him there was an " ideal summer " blowing
through his brain, there was " a nature behind
the common, unexplored by science or by literature " which, like the plumage of the red election
bird, he hoped would " assume stranger and more
dazzling colors, like the tints of morning, in proportion as I advanced further into the darkness
and solitude of the forest." He was ever expect-
ing greater things ; " we have hardly entered the
vestibule of Nature," he believed. He had a passionate desire to exhibit his strange love as she
dressed for him, to reproduce these absolutely
strange elements of Nature in literature. Lowell's
earliest judgments,[1] of Thoreau that " generally
he holds a very smooth mirror up to nature," and
of his literary achievement that " Melville's pictures of life in Typee have no attraction beside
it," by no means did justice to Thoreau's effort.
Nor did Henry James's patronizing notice of " his
remarkable genius for flinging a kind of spiritual interest over these things [birds and beasts
and trees] " strike the center. John Burroughs
questions Thoreau's sincerity : " If Thoreau had

[1] *Pertaining to Thoreau* (ed. S. A. Jones, Detroit, 1901), pp.
21, 23.

made friends with a dog to share his bed and
board in his retreat by Walden Pond, one would
have had more faith in his sincerity. The dog
would have been the seal and authentication of his
retreat. A man who has no heart for a dog, —
how can he have a heart for Nature herself?"
But Mr. Burroughs has never been quite able to
understand what Thoreau was doing, and has been
content to observe that "he put the whole of
Nature between himself and his fellows"; forget-
ting that for Thoreau there were no "fellows,"
and only one love.

Thoreau informed a friend in 1841 that Nature was "more human than any single man or
woman can be." In those early days such a remark amounted in Thoreau to little more than
a pleasantry, an exercise in paradox. Then Nature was mere mild "Alma Natura," and meant
mainly health to Thoreau. But very soon he is
"struck with the pleasing friendships and una-
nimities of Nature, as when the lichen on the
trees takes the form of their leaves." Some
years later he finds himself a party to such a
"unanimity": "My acquaintances sometimes
imply that I am too cold; but each thing is warm
enough of its kind. . . . You who complain
that I am cold find Nature cold. To me she is
warm." [1] "If I am too cold for human friend-

[1] *Journal*, III, 147.

ship, I trust I shall not soon be too cold for natural influences. It appears to be a law that you cannot have a deep sympathy with both man and nature. Those qualities which bring you near to the one estrange you from the other."[1] At Walden he finds that " every little pine needle expanded and swelled with sympathy and befriended me "; and in 1854 he is heard at his distance asserting, " I cannot spare my moonlight and my mountains for the best of men I am likely to get in exchange." " Because joy is withered away from the sons of men," and because friends of the perfect sort are not to be found among the sons of men, he hastens to play the " welcome guest " to Nature. " Who shall criticise that companion ? " Did not their atmospheres mingle? Was not she wild enough to be a neighbor? Was not she staid and settled for life? Was not she minding her own business superbly? Was he not she? was she not he? Did not she give all that he demanded? " I love nature, because it never cheats me. It never jests. It is cheerfully, musically earnest," he wrote in a kind of desperation. Was it not altogether possible to cherish his " idea " of friendship in the company of Nature? Did not Nature hold out to him the only hope of assurance that life was yet joyful when he saw slavery in Massachusetts? With his friends disappearing over the rim of his little — or big — world, was not Nature left? If men dwelt nowhere, were there not fields still to traverse? Who could " communicate immortality" to him better than Nature?

"All nature is my bride," announced Thoreau in 1857.[1] The bride and groom, it seems, had been children together. "Henry talks about Nature just as if she'd been born and brought up in Concord," observed Madam Hoar. Nature was as faithful a consort to Thoreau as Ocean was to Melville's Moby Dick: "Almost universally," says Melville, "a lone whale proves an ancient one. Like venerable moss-bearded Daniel Boone, he will have no one near him but Nature herself; and her he takes to wife in the wilderness of waters, and the best of wives she is, though she keeps so many moody secrets." The two died together, perhaps: "When he had wakeful nights," writes Sophia Thoreau, " he would ask me to arrange the furniture so as to make fantastic shadows on the wall, and he wished his bed was in the form of a shell that he might curl up in it."

When it is said that Thoreau found in Nature his ideal friend, it is meant that he found in her his complete sympathizer. Hawthorne, who as a

[1] *Journal*, ix, 337.

young man interviewed Thoreau, "said that
Thoreau prided himself on coming nearer the
heart of a pine-tree than any other human being."
Thoreau has much to say concerning this affinity. "Friendship is the unspeakable joy and
blessing that results to two or more individuals
who from constitution sympathize. . . . Who
are the estranged? Two friends explaining."[1]
"Friendship takes place between those who have
an affinity for one another and is a perfectly
natural and regular event." "It is hard to know
rocks. They are crude and inaccessible to our
nature. We have not enough of the stony element in us." Nature, thought Thoreau, could
always be trusted by one who had this affinity
for her; perhaps it was because the affinity between himself and Nature had not yet become
complete that on a certain day, after long deliberation and many trials at a mutual understanding, he spanked a woodchuck which would
keep pestering his premises.

It is easy to see where Thoreau wished all
the sympathy to be. "In the whole school," says
Lowell, speaking of Rousseau and the European
sentimentalists, "there is a sickly taint . . . a
sensibility to the picturesque in Nature, not with
Nature as a strengthener and consoler, a wholesome tonic for a mind ill at ease with itself, but

[1] *Journal*, III, 146.

with Nature as a kind of feminine echo to the mood, flattering it with sympathy rather than correcting it with rebuke or lifting it away from its unmanly depression, as in the wholesomer fellow-feeling of Wordsworth." In Thoreau there is also a taint, though it is scarcely a "sickly" or an "unmanly" taint. Emerson, who pronounced that "in fine the ancient precept, 'Know thyself,' and the modern precept, 'Study Nature,' become at last one maxim," was himself tainted with mad (if manly) intellectual egoism. And Thoreau, who always went one step farther than Emerson, went here also one step farther. When one of Thoreau's critics went into forest retirement for two years, he found his imagination "awed and purified" by contact with Nature, and found that great peace of mind was the fruit of the fellowship — peace in the presence of Nature's great, calm, "passionless power." [1] He considered then that Nature to Thoreau had also been a "discipline of the will as much as a stimulant to the imagination." This is true only with a reservation; Thoreau's will ran free of discipline to the extent that his intellect ran wild in Nature; and there was little else than intellect in him (as in the other transcendental essayists) to discipline. "He had

[1] Paul Elmer More, "A Hermit's Notes on Thoreau," *Shelburne Essays*, I.

no temptations to fight against — no appetites, no passions," Emerson said. He lived, indeed, quite outside the circle of Good and Bad. When Thoreau told himself in 1841,[1] "I exult in stark inanity, leering on nature and the soul," he surely was launching forth on no career of strict self-supervision. As early as 1842 he was recommending the forest to the readers of the "Dial" for no other reason than that "the solitary rambler may find a response and expression for every mood" in its depth. He refused to like men because they begrudged him indefinite expansion in their direction;[2] and came to like Nature because Nature expected nothing of him. "What a hero one can be without moving a finger!" he exclaimed at twenty-one. He might have exclaimed in 1850, "What a lover of Nature one can be without conceding a mood!" His ideal was independence; Nature never criticized him. His ideal demanded something absolutely to be trusted, capable of any interpretation, inexhaustible to any curious mind, giving all and taking nothing, yet not complaining of the sacrifice; Nature was all that.

Thoreau can be very grandly condemned for seeking himself in Nature. But his successors in the poet-naturalist rôle can be condemned yet more for seeking themselves in Nature. One

[1] *Journal*, I, 175.   [2] *Ibid.*, IX, 209.

cannot say that Thoreau was a better man than they, or a stronger; Nature is neither good nor bad, neither strong nor weak. One can say that Thoreau is vastly more interesting than they. At least he is the only one of them all whose personality is intrinsically so interesting that people will long be interested in preserving the books in which it is reflected on Nature's mirror.

Thoreau himself despised what he called " the mealy-mouthed enthusiasm of the [mere] lover of nature." One smiles to think what he would say in these latter days. He would deplore the exploitation by nature-fakers and nature-hacks of the pathetic fallacy in their animal stories. He would be monstrously impatient with the poor " nature-study" of bird books and tree books, which prefers quite harmless and quite useless curiosity to dangerous or quite useful speculation. He would say that modern nature books insult the intelligence, and are gauged for a race of school-children. He would not flatly agree that " one must live until tired, and think until baffled, before he can know his need of Nature," or that all one goes to the woods for is to find a place where he can " know without thinking." He would have veneration for the manly and painstaking John Burroughs, but he would agree that he is no poet. He would be unspeakably sickened by the hot hysteria in the books of

Richard Jefferies, with their " insatiable yearning for a full, rich life," their effeminate groping for a newer " series of ideas " and a newer " range of thought " than those which have exercised the world for five thousand years, — or five million, — their morbid fidgeting to be " plunged deep in existence," their sad conviction that " there is something more than existence," their unfledged talk of " soul-culture," their total want of originality, their spiritual sterility. If one seeks a point of difference between Thoreau and Jefferies, he need read no further than this sentence in the latter's " Story of my Life": " I should like to be loved by every beautiful woman on earth from the swart Nubian to the white and divine Greek."

Further comparisons are of no value. " After all," said Walt Whitman, reflecting once on the difference between the relations to Nature of Burroughs and Thoreau, " I suppose outdoors had nothing to do with that difference. The contrast just shows what sort of men Thoreau and Burroughs were to start with." It has been seen that Thoreau's ideal of the friendly relation demanded complete sympathy and toleration from the second party. It has been seen that he found no such friend among mankind, went therefore to Nature, and was satisfied with her companionship. When Nature was about to slay his body

with consumption, he was not resentful. She still
was friend to what he believed to be the real part
of him, his mind ; she still permitted him to think
whatever he pleased. This exaggerated confidence
in his own mind was what Thoreau had to start
with.

III

A WHIMSICAL passage in the Journal for 1856[1] intimates the character of the demands which Thoreau made upon the universe and which no friend save Nature could meet: —

" Aug. 31. Sunday, P.M. — To Hubbard Bath Swamp by boat.

" There sits one by the shore who wishes to go with me, but I cannot think of it. I must be fancy-free. There is no such mote in the sky as a man who is not perfectly transparent to you, — who has any opacity. I would rather attend to him earnestly for half an hour, on shore or else-where, and then dismiss him. He thinks I could merely take him into my boat and then not mind him. He does not realize that I should by the same act take him into my mind, where there is no room for him, and my bark would surely founder in such a voyage as I was contemplating. I know very well that I should never reach that expansion of the river I have in my mind, with him aboard with his broad terrene qualities. He would sink my bark (not to another sea) and never know it. I could better carry a heaped load

[1] *Journal*, IX, 46.

of meadow mud and sit on the thole-pins. There
would be more room for me, and I should reach
that expansion of the river nevertheless. . . .
These things are settled by fate. The good ship
sails — when she is ready. . . . What is getting
into a man's carriage when it is full, compared
with putting your foot in his mouth and popping
right into his mind without considering whether
it is occupied or not? . . . Often, I would rather
undertake to shoulder a barrel of pork and carry
it a mile than take into my company a man. It
would not be so heavy a weight upon my mind.
I could put it down and only feel my *back* ache
for it."

"Let us know our limits," proposed Pascal.
For Thoreau, expansion beyond all limits was the
one thing needful. Friends are a weary weight,
companions are a burden. He maintained aus-
terely, like the Oriental philosopher, that " perfect benevolence does not admit the feeling of
affection. . . . Perfect benevolence is the very
highest thing. . . . It is difficult to forget all the
men in the world." His idea of a friend was
" some broad and generous natural person, as
frank as the daylight, in whose presence our behavior will be as simple and unconstrained as
the wanderer amid the recesses of these hills." [1]
To be friends two persons must be something

[1] *Journal*, i, 442.

inhuman like the elements — the daylight — to each other, must have universes that coincide. The circles must not intersect. He morbidly demanded, as " the essence of friendship," " a total magnanimity and trust." " What Henry Thoreau needed," said one who knew him, " was to be believed in through thick and thin and then let alone." He asked for the privilege, not of loving, but of admiring, and he exercised man's prerogative, not in being hurt, but in being disgusted. Mr. Howells says it was a " John Brown type, a John Brown ideal, a John Brown principle," for which he was protagonist, and not a man John Brown. The sympathy he called for was of a higher strain than that in which most men sympathize. It was a sympathy of which the mind could make any disposition it chose; it could be exercised on fish as legitimately as on men; and it was to be paid for only by toleration, agreement, veneration.

It has been supposed that the experiment with a community at Brook Farm suggested to Thoreau the other experiment of perfecting man in solitude. Thoreau, it is more correct to say, was born possessed with the demon of expansion, and much more radically so than the reader only of " Walden," with its witty digs at busybodies and its droll defense of loneliness, can realize. " Every man should stand for a force which is

perfectly irresistible," he wrote to a friend in
1848. " How can any man be weak who dares to
be at all? . . . What a wedge, what a beetle,
what a catapult, is an *earnest* man! What can
resist him?" Emerson lamented that Thoreau
did not let his uncommon energy play in action.
It did play and quiver within him steadily in
pure, vacuous expansion. "My most essential
progress must be to me a state of absolute rest,"
announced Thoreau, for whom absolute rest was
absolute action, and " engineering for all America" were pure waste of time. If a note in nineteenth-century romantic thought was the note of
natural human expansion, Thoreau in that century, on tiptoe like chanticleer, stands himself
for pure expansion of the pure self. If the expansion of Chateaubriand was an expansion of
the religious sensibilities, if that of Wordsworth
was benevolent, if that of Ruskin was æsthetic,
if that of Emerson was intellectual, that of Thoreau was most purely egoistic. "The cost of a
thing," says he, " is the amount of what I call
life [and what others might call self-satisfaction]
which is required to be exchanged for it." There
was in Thoreau a rage for self-satisfaction, not
always to be appeased. Stevenson says, "He had
not enough of the superficial, even at command."
He fled the superficial for "centrality," and
wanted centrality as a caged lion wants liberty.

" As long as possible live free and uncommitted," he advised in " Walden." All he asked was to be let alone. As early as his twentieth year he was saying in a college oration, " The characteristic of our epoch is perfect freedom — freedom of thought and action "; and twelve years later he was telling himself that " The only obligation which I have a right to assume is to do at any time what I think right." He asked for elbow-room because he never knew in advance in what direction he might have to expand : " I have no more distinctness or pointedness in my yearnings than an expanding bud. . . . I feel ripe for something, yet do nothing, can't discover what that thing is. I feel fertile merely." This testiness and this mere fertility are far from being the pleasant qualities of Thoreau. Stevenson says, " Thoreau is dry, priggish, and selfish," and has " none of that large, unconscious geniality of the world's heroes " — probably a just judgment. " A call from Thoreau in the highest sense meant business," and " he was on his guard not to be over-influenced," acquaintances reported. It is impossible to imagine at times a more relentless or a more disagreeable expansion.

Expansion of the pure self explains Thoreau's attitude toward collective society. Alcott considered him " the best republican citizen in the world, — always at home, and minding his own affairs." Certainly the troubles of mankind caused him no disturbance. He was as steadfastly and religiously self-centered as Cardinal Newman was concerned for the personal soul when Newman held it "better for the sun and moon to drop from heaven, for the earth to fail, and for all the many millions on it to die of starvation in extremest agony, as far as temporal affliction goes, than that one soul, I will not say should be lost, but should commit one venial sin." Thoreau believed, indeed, that God was with him; "God does not sympathize with the popular movements," he said. He had a Nietzschean contempt for the "gregariousness" of men; assemblies of men he said he saw only as assemblies of animals with broad flapping ears. Defying the fourth chapter of Ecclesiastes, he permitted himself to describe society as "pigs in a litter, which lie close together to keep each other warm";[1] and opposed Fourierism because it asked men to stand propped against one another rather than planted, each one firmly, in the eternal. A curt passage in the "Maine Woods" reflects best, perhaps, if vicariously, Thoreau's own contempt for the intercourse of men: "We had been told in Bangor of a man who lived alone, a sort of hermit, at the dam, to

[1] *Journal*, IV, 397.

take care of it, who spent his time tossing a bullet from one hand to the other for want of employment. . . . This sort of tit-for-tat intercourse between his two hands, bandying to and fro a leaden object, seems to have been his symbol for society."

The course of Thoreau's career in expansion is interesting. From the first he stood apart. Says a college mate, " The touch of his hand was moist and indifferent, as if he had taken up something when he saw your hand coming — and caught your grasp upon it." From the first he had determined to grow perfect after his own fashion. " What a hero one can be without moving a finger ! " But not until the rather listless and aimless Thoreau who left college was energized by the spirit of Emerson, not until his remarkable essay, " The Service, or Qualities of the Recruit," written about 1840, perhaps in answer to the " discourses on Peace and Non-Resistance which in 1840 were so numerous in New England,"[1] and left unprinted in full till the edition of 1902, does Thoreau's policy of spherical expansion find words[2] : " We shall not attain to be spherical by lying on one or the other side for an eternity, but only by resigning ourselves implicitly to the law of gravity in us, shall we find our axis coincident with the celes-

[1] *The Service* (ed. F. B. Sanborn), p. vii.   [2] *Ibid.*, p. 6.

tial axis, and by revolving incessantly through all circles, acquire a perfect sphericity. . . . The brave man is a perfect sphere, which cannot fall on its flat side, and is equally strong every way." The recruit in the ranks of the Eternal can dispense with bravado before the world: "The coward wants resolution, which the brave man can do without. . . . His [the brave man's] bravery deals not so much in resolute action, as healthy and assured rest; its palmy state is a staying at home and compelling alliance in all directions." Here is the last word needed to prove that Thoreau from the first was self-appointed to expand spherically at the expense of the world's gifts — friendship, love, fame. Perhaps more of the essential Thoreau can be seen in "The Service" than in any other twenty-five pages of him.

ᵗᵒ p. 109

Thoreau, then, embarks upon his voyage of expansion. "It is time now that I begin to live," he tells himself in 1841.[1] When he goes to Ktaadn he is reassured to find that the forest owl is "plainly not nervous about his solitary life." In 1850 he writes of accidentally setting fire to some woods, and so destroying the property of several farmers; but he is more concerned for himself than for the farmers, since the woods have been *his* friend, the boundary of *his* visible sphere. In 1851 his harvest of satisfaction does

[1] *Journal*, I, 299.

not appear so rich as he had expected : " Here I
am thirty-four years old, and yet my life is almost
wholly unexpanded. How much is in the germ!" [1]
He notices in alarm that " the character of my
knowledge is from year to year becoming more distinct and scientific ; that, in exchange for views as
wide as heaven's cope, I am being narrowed down
to the field of the microscope." But he decides that
he has perhaps contracted " a fatal coarseness " as
the "result of mixing in the trivial affairs of men,"
and decides that human wishes are intrinsically
and inevitably vain : " The youth gets together
his materials to build a bridge to the moon, or
perchance a palace or temple on the earth, and at
length the middle-aged man concludes to build a
wood-shed with them." He takes Nature now to
wife, and henceforth alternates between doubt
that his expansion is bearing the fruit for which
his appetite was set and overemphatic self-assurance. In 1853 he looks back wistfully to riper
days when he grew like corn in the night : " Ah,
those youthful days! Are they never to return ?
When the walker does not too curiously observe
particulars, but sees, hears, scents, tastes, and
feels only himself, . . . his expanding body, his
intellect and heart. . . . The unbounded universe
was his. A bird is now become a mote in his
eye." But he secures himself again at Walden,

[1] *Journal*, II, 316.

whither he had gone most confidently to "front
only the essential facts of life": "I learned this,
at least, by my experiment: that if one advances
confidently in the direction of his dreams, and
endeavors to live the life which he has imagined,
he will meet with success unexpected in common
hours." By 1856 he is willing to concede that the
fruit of expansion may be slight and intangible
after all: "Let not your life be wholly without
an object, though it be only to ascertain the
flavor of a cranberry, for it will not be only the
quality of an insignificant berry that you will
have tasted, but the flavor of your life to that
extent, and it will be such a sauce as no wealth
can buy."[1] Life by 1857 is empty to Thoreau
beside the life he sketched in "The Service":
"In proportion as death is more earnest than life,
it is better than life." In 1858 "the truth com-
pels me to regard the ideal and the actual as two
things."[2] As early as 1849 Thoreau had observed[3]
that perhaps the tang in the wild apple's flavor
was the one thing real, and could "make my ap-
parently poor life rich." In the last few years, and
particularly after the John Brown episode, this
tang is the only solace in solitude, the only justi-
fication for fastidiousness, is all that remains in
Thoreau's universe, one is tempted to conclude.
The necessity of wildness is all he can declaim

[1] *Journal*, ix, 37.   [2] *Familiar Letters*, 332.   [3] *Ibid.*, 174.

on in " Walking." In the ninth volume of the " Journal" he hints that "life is barely tolerable " at times.

Coming from the pure mysticism of "The Service," through the practical self-assurance of " Walden," down through the tortuous mysticism of the later Journal, to drain the cup of expansion, Thoreau finds the dregs to be a single shriveled sensation. The lion in his cage purred contentedly in 1840 ; breathed easily and deeply in pastoral sphericity in the nature essays of 1842 and 1843 ; swelled opulently and confidently in the " Week"; began to prowl along the walls and sniff in apprehension at the locks in " Walden " ; chased off all intruders next; lay down, sore and annoyed, during the slavery debates ; rose up and struck out with his paw once when prodded ; lay down again in the end to sniff Eternity for tang. Timon is shrunk indeed.

If Thoreau was born with the germ of expansion within him, where did he find an external, a philosophical, sanction ? Who else preached sphericity before him ? Who gave him words and ideas with which to announce his programme and report his progress ?

The expansion seed certainly took wing in the beginning from transcendental Germany. But transcendentalism is one thing, and romanticism is another. It has never been determined just how much the movement which grew out of German transcendentalism and which is called German romanticism had to do with American transcendental expansion. It has been suggested that "the transcendental philosophy of New England had absorbed the language and ideas of German romanticism, if not its inmost spirit";[1] and that the formulæ of the school may have been transmitted to America through the magazines. It is true that there are not a few of the romantic marks on the Americans. Emerson, in the "English Traits," said, "The Germans think for Europe"; Emerson had been given more than an outline of the German programme by Coleridge. Even before the time of the romanticists, Zimmermann, a German Rousseauist, had sent forth some of their ideas in his widely popular "Thoughts on the Influence of Solitude on the Heart," and this book ran through ten editions in America between 1793 and 1825;[2] Daniel Ricketson, Thoreau's friend, had a copy in his shanty when Thoreau visited him in 1857.[3] Thoreau himself bears some resemblance to the German romanticists; for him too "paradox was the fine flower

[1] Paul Elmer More, "Thoreau and German Romanticism," *Shelburne Essays*, v.

[2] W. C. Goodnight, *German Literature in American Magazines prior to 1846.* University of Wisconsin, 1909.

[3] *Journal*, ix, 324. A memorandum by Thoreau of the books in his library in 1840 (with later additions) shows that he also owned a copy of Zimmermann's book, printed in Albany.

of thought." The Germans too decried " extreme busyness," contemned the professions, and despised politics. Novalis was made much of in the " Dial "; and Thoreau worships Night now and then like a Novalis. It has been claimed more than once that the parable of the hound, the bay horse, and the turtle-dove is a direct reminiscence of Novalis and so of Germany.

But the suggestion for that parable might have come, the " Dial " shows, from an Oriental Bible in an English translation. And it is thinkable that most of the so-called resemblances between the Americans and the Germans are no more than the inevitable resemblances between kindred minds trained on the same theme. While it can be said that the German influence on English and American speculation was profound, it can be said with equal foundation that any speculation is more or less profound *per se*, and does not always ask for full instructions from without. A certain passage from Emerson's Journal for 1849 may reinforce that point:[1] " Mr. Scherb [a German exile in Concord] attempted last night to unfold Hegel for me, and I caught somewhat that seemed cheerful and large, and that might, and probably did, come by Hindoo suggestion. But all abstract philosophy is easily anticipated, — it is so structural, or necessitated by the mould of the human mind." Any one who has begun a

[1] Emerson's *Journal*, viii, 69. 1849.

"structural" philosophy like Spinoza's appreciates that only a hint — the first definition — is needed to set the mind careering at once through the whole system unaided.

It may be worth while to experiment with a typical American transcendental interest, and measure how much of German influence it shows. It can be shown that the Americans, and particularly Thoreau, got their Oriental enthusiasm, not from the Germans, but directly from their own philosophical needs and indirectly from England. Thoreau himself had not a free use of German,[1] and had no enthusiasm for it. The books sent him by his English friend Cholmondeley were " English, French, Latin, Greek, and Sanskrit." The Oriental books which Thoreau bequeathed to Emerson[2] were in English and French. In the prefaces to his selections from the Oriental Scriptures in the " Dial " Thoreau cites only English editions — by Colebrooke, Jones, Hodgson, Collie, Wilson, or Wilkins. He need not have gone outside his Chalmers's " Poets," which he read without skipping, to come under the enthusiastic Sir William Jones's influence ; Jones's Oriental poems and " Essay on the Poetry of the Eastern Nations" were printed there.

[1] F. B. Sanborn, *The Personality of Thoreau* (1906), p. 36.
[2] Emerson's *Journal*, ix, 419.

By what chance Thoreau came to read the Orientals, or what editions he read, is of less consequence, perhaps, than why they were congenial, and who interested him in them. The encouragement to this reading, it would seem, came solely from Emerson and thence from England — always, of course, against the broad background of European transcendental assertion of the moral and intellectual dignity of man. Emerson, " who, bland angel as he was, very much wanted his own way," " invented or elected his philosophy," one of the most careful of writers has said.[1] And it is perfectly reasonable to agree that, born with a capacious mind, moved by the sentiment of intellectuality, enchanted by glimpses into Coleridge's bottomless intellect, quick to accept Coleridge's policy of reflection for reflection's sake, and committed to comprehensiveness of intellect as the definition and goal of genius, Emerson might have gone quite independently, and not as an impoverished borrower, to whatever works seemed to him profound, and have taken away what caprice or plan dictated. Emerson owned one of the first copies of the " Bhagavad-Gîtâ " in America;[2] he lent it freely; and he got it read much more widely than the Harvard Library copy was read. It was

[1] W. C. Brownell, " Emerson," *American Prose Masters.*
[2] *Nation* (New York), May 12, 1910, p. 481.

to English or French scholars, and not to German scholars, that the American transcendentalists went — Jones, Colebrooke, Mackintosh, Wilson, Wilkins, Lee, Wilford, Marshman, and Collie, descendants of a long line of purely English Orientalists hailing from the fourteenth century. German and English scholars of the early nineteenth century vied with each other for recognition as inspirers of European Oriental enthusiasm. The matter can hardly be settled. It is enough to show that Emerson's and Thoreau's Orientalism could have been an independent growth on English soil.

The point has been made that Thoreau received the breath of the German philosophy, but "always . . . with differences caused by other surroundings and traditions."[1] These differences are really more interesting than the resemblance itself. The two schools are exactly alike in that they preach infinite expansion of self. But when it is considered that the Americans lived what they thought, as Novalis did not ; that the aspiration of the Americans was as much for a whole people as it was for their æsthetic selves ; that the Germans often, the Americans never, inclined to the fleshly, — it is easy to see very important details of dissimilarity. There is a

[1] Paul Elmer More, " The Centenary of Longfellow," *Shelburne Essays*, v.

greater difference than any of those. The expansion of the Germans was emotional; that of the Americans was intellectual. And Thoreau took his cue, not from Germany at all, but from America; he took it from the New England intellectual renaissance and from Emerson, who himself was much more a Platonist than he was a German idealist.[1]

"No truer American ever lived," said Emerson. Probably no one not a Yankee could have written so shrewd and yet so earnest a book as "Walden." Thoreau at least was writing what he believed to be the truth for America, and not solely what pleased his own fancy; he did not want to live alone merely to be eccentric, but that he might be normal — to the brim a normal American. And to be a normal American in 1840 was neither to have forgotten one's Puritan heritage nor to have failed to cast one's self in with the intellectually emancipated. De Tocqueville said that the Americans were a nation without neighbors, and given to moral self-contemplation. By 1840 New England had by no means forgotten the profound religious experiences of such men as Cotton, Wheelwright, Vane, Penn, John Woolman, Jonathan Edwards, Nicholas Gilman, and Samuel Hopkins; nor had it forgotten Puritanism, the firmness of whose estab-

[1] J. H. Harrison, *The Teachers of Emerson.* (1910.)

lishment in even Thoreau's transcendental mind
is attested by the fact that he denounced what
he did not believe in — for example, money —
as not only foolish but sinful. It was that ances-
tral Puritan voice that made Thoreau hearken
to Confucius when he recommended " blameless-
ness of life," or " simple truth and earnestness."
Neither was he unaware that a veritable renaissance of intellect had set in in New England
during his boyhood, and that what he called
" brain rot " was on the way to being cured.
New England itself had subscribed to sphericity.
Conscious of new spiritual liberty and nearly
isolated from Europe during the thirty years of
comparative international quiet following the
Napoleonic wars, coming in that period to take
account of its intellectual stock and finding it
slim, craving a spiritual exaltation commensur-
able with the new territorial and numerical expansion of America, and piqued by such insults
from Europe as Sydney Smith's poser in the
" Edinburgh Review " in 1820 — " Who reads
an American Book ? " — it was inevitable that
some of the doughtier spirits should propose to
wage a grim spiritual campaign. Such spirits,
wearing self-reliance for a charm, and deplor-
ing the meaner " busyness " of their fellow citi-
zens, must have tired of " bargain and corrup-
tion " politics, must have scorned to notice the

twenty-nine benevolent and charitable institutions that had grown up in Boston between 1810 and 1840, must have disdained Fourier and Albert Brisbane, and the Society for the Diffusion of Useful Knowledge, must have held fastidious noses up above the penny newspapers which tried to be all things to all men and were, it was charged, not very much of one thing to any.

Specifically, Thoreau's doctrine of sphericity came from Emerson. Emerson, optimistically announcing that "all things show that on every side we are very near to the best"; Emerson, preaching his philosophy of "circles" with unrivaled zeal; Emerson, declaring that "there is no end in Nature, but every end is a beginning; that there is always another dawn risen on midnoon, and under every deep a lower deep opens"; Emerson, having it that "the only sin is limitation," caught and held and made Thoreau — or, as one man had it, "ruined" him. "No one meeting Emerson was ever the same again." Perhaps a conversation with Emerson furnished Thoreau a hint for "The Service," for Emerson wrote this in his essay "Character": "The face which character wears to me is self-sufficingness . . . character is centrality, the impossibility of being displaced or overset." It is possible that Thoreau saw a challenge in Emerson's essay, "The Transcendentalist" in the "Dial" for

1842, which contained a clause, "There is no pure Transcendentalist." Emerson has much to say upon the relations between his ideas and Thoreau's: "Thoreau gives me, in flesh and blood and pertinacious Saxon belief, my own ethics. He is far more real, and daily practically obeying them, than I."[1] "I am very familiar with all his thoughts, — they are my own quite originally drest."[2] Certainly Thoreau's ideas of Nature, Love, Friendship, Sphericity, are Emerson's — Emerson's pointed and trimmed with Thoreau's tools. And certainly, with Emerson's wide reading in Herbert, Henry More, Milton, Coleridge, Thomas Taylor, Plato, Plotinus, and the Oriental Scriptures at hand, Thoreau did not need to look to Germany for intellectual day. He had with him always one of the best examples of the intellectual gormandizer the world has seen.

When Thoreau's most discriminating critic[3] defines the larger differences between Thoreau and the Germans, he implies that Thoreau was, upon the whole, not altogether as rapacious for expansion as were the Germans. Thus, finding on both the marks of romanticism, "aloofness," "irony," "sacred idleness," "musical revery," "communion with Nature," and "contempt for limitations," he goes on to say for Thoreau that

---

[1] Emerson's *Journal*, VIII, 303.   [2] *Ibid.*, VI, 74.
[3] More, "Thoreau and German Romanticism."

because he expanded from the base of character and intellect rather than from the base of sensibility and the flesh, he therefore exercised his will for discipline of self, exercised a " higher self-restraint." The critic suggests that several intermediary influences are responsible for this element of restraint in the American, — " the inheritance of the Puritan religion," " the British notion of practical individualism," " the lesson of Wordsworth's austerity in the devotion to Nature," the " spirit of fine expectancy " in the seventeenth-century poets, the " incalculable force of Emerson's personality "; and one might add the discipline of the classics, the discipline of manual labor, and the example of the Indian race. It can be questioned whether the difference between the Germans and Thoreau was the difference between men who exercised no restraint at all and a man who exercised a " higher self-restraint." It is no evidence in Thoreau's favor that he, with all the transcendentalists, dealt all the while in " character " and " intellect," or that he lived in a " dry light." Further glances into the Journal and other localities will reveal what use Thoreau and Emerson made of the terms " intellect " and " character," and what actually came of Thoreau's " dry light."

There is no evidence that Emerson and Thoreau believed in training or did train their intel-

lects; there is no end of evidence that they en-
gaged instead in a very noble and care-free kind
of intellectual debauch and indulged what has
been styled their "intellectual pride and moral
confidence" to the mortal limit. "There is no
past in the soul" — no building of ideas — said
Thoreau. They believed heart and soul in doing
as one likes, in being as good as one can in any
way one likes, and in thinking as industriously
as one can in any direction he fancies. *Spes
sibi quisque*, from Virgil, was Thoreau's motto
for "The Service." Thoreau went out to Walden Pond in order to "have a little world all
to himself" . . . "not cumbered and mortified
by his memory." Emerson and Thoreau had
ideals; their ideals were themselves. They were
intellectual and moral, but intellectual and moral
all to themselves. They cared to be conscious of
no limits. "Who," asks Thoreau in "Walking,"
"but the Evil One has cried Whoa! to mankind?" The "spirit of fine expectancy" of the
seventeenth-century poets would not have owned
New England in 1850. Herbert's face was turned
upward; Emerson's and Thoreau's faces inward.
Herbert pleaded with God for vision; Emerson
and Thoreau only pricked themselves perpetually on to further spiritual adventures. Herbert's
"morning" was that time of man's life when
he is permitted to forget himself and glimpse

the universal order. Emerson's and Thoreau's "morning" was a perpetual period in which men should be "awake" — that is, have "life, and knowledge" of themselves. The self-conscious, thin patriarchal integrity they thought they had reclaimed from civilization the patriarchs would not recognize at all.

Emerson and Thoreau led a headlong revolt against "natural" sympathy only to plunge into shoreless seas of intellectual and moral egotism. Mind-intoxicated men, cutting their own channels, thinking as they pleased, keeping their foreheads smooth, hungry for ideas and uncritical of ideas when they come along, dreading to repeat themselves, needing "infinite room" to utter their thoughts in, musing to satiety, boasting native potential omniscience, refusing to argue but eager to declaim, never comparing but always uttering, setting thought above knowledge and instinct above reflection, more hospitable to thoughts than to men, they furnish beautiful examples of the behavior of wild nature in intellect. Thinking to defy Hume's conclusions concerning "the weakness of human reason, and the narrow limits to which it is confined," they denied any limits whatever. As Ruskin said, " Men are as their tastes," and Carlyle said, " Men are as they are strong," so these said, " Men are as they think boundlessly." Fondly imagining their intellectual system to be organized on the grandest possible ultimate plan, they careered on with no immediate organization whatever; identifying "centrality" of Emersonian thought with universal gravitation, they believed themselves safe and sped on after new sensations. With no conception of that kind of intellectual organization which Newman, for one, demanded, they tore on their way to flaunt endlessly those faculties which Newman shuddered to contemplate — " fierce, wilful human nature," " the wild living intellect of man," " the immense energy of the aggressive, capricious, untrustworthy intellect."

Neither Emerson nor Thoreau was free from the intellectual demon; neither Emerson nor Thoreau escaped those intellectual perils which are inevitably contingent upon so fatally easy a system as theirs and which have been visible since among the Christian Scientists. Neither Emerson nor Thoreau wound up his intellectual career with half the satisfaction that he began it. That was not possible when their procedure was so prodigal. Thoreau is to be seen, as early as his college days, recommending the keeping of a Journal in order to conserve one's thoughts and to be able to oversee one's mind ; and he declares that thoughts come " spontaneously," " suggest themselves." An intellectual epicure at twenty,

he is an intellectual hero at thirty, when he says,
" All I can say is that I live and breathe and
have my thoughts," and when he believes that
" to know, is to know good." [1] Miss Fuller said
she " had a pleasant time with her mind." So
Thoreau in his prime played with his mind. He
tells, in the Journal for 1851,[2] how " I had a
thought this morning before I awoke. I endeav-
ored to retain it in my mind's grasp after I became conscious, yet I doubted, while I lay on my
back, whether my mind could apprehend it when
I should stand erect. It is a . . . difficult feat to
get up without spilling your morning thought."
Certain parts of the Journal breathe no such self-
satisfaction as this. There are to be read what
for Thoreau are long, incoherent passages which
betray that, along with his loss of confidence in
sphericity and his unspoken pain at the loss of
friends, he suffered pretty frequently a diminu-
tion of that " hard mentality," that " grip and
exactitude of mind," that " mental materialism "
which Emerson praised in George Herbert. Here
is no noble mind overthrown ; but here are mental gifts squandered somewhat from want of
shaping and direction.

If Thoreau had been in truth what Emerson
believed him, and what he may have wished to

---

[1] " Natural History of Massachusetts," *Excursions.*
[2] *Journal,* iii, 121.

believe himself, a "perfect piece of stoicism,"
there would have been shaping of a kind; but
one cannot detect a note of genuine stoicism in
all of him. One cannot confuse Thoreau with
Marcus Aurelius, falling back on Providence
and universal philanthropy. Thoreau was not
weary of life, saw nothing in it to hide, heard
nothing in it that should be talked down. He
surrendered himself to no universal law he could
not understand, resigned himself to nothing he
did not like. He was no "strong and noble
spirit contending against odds." His philosophy
was no "reaction against chronic anxiety." Thoreau liked to think that he was something of a
Cato, and read, it seems pretty carefully, in
Cato, Varro, and Columella. But there is a vast
difference between the citizen Cato and the sentimentalist Thoreau. Cato embraced simplicity
as a duty; Thoreau embraced it as a luxury.
Cato lived in Rome; Thoreau lived in "a little
world of his own." Cato had a rough, sensible
Lincolnian humor; Thoreau priggishly exor-
cised humor from his books. Thoreau extravagantly claimed everything for solitude; of Cato,
Livy says, *Nulla ars neque privatæ neque pub-
licæ rei gerendæ ei defuit*.

Thoreau was an out-and-out Epicurean. It is
not true that he "wanted little." He wanted
everything. Stevenson says he "loved to in-

dulge the mind rather than the body," and was
" an Epicurean of the nobler sort," — " cruel in
the pursuit of goodness, morbid in the pursuit
of health . . . that valetudinarian healthfulness
which is more delicate than sickness itself."
" Economy is the second or third cousin of Ava-
rice," goes the proverb. Thoreau's absolute sense
of security in the world was not stoical but epicurean ; he said, " A man should feed his senses
on the best the land affords." Marcus Aurelius
was a Stoic because he kept an inner self to
which he could retire for ease and reassurance in
the midst of a distressed life. Thoreau avoided
a distressed life in order to have perpetual peace,
to monopolize his inner self. The world could
not seem hard to him, because he was padded
on all sides by his ego. He wrote, in " The
Service," " Necessity is my eastern cushion on
which I recline. . . . I ask no more but to be
left alone with it. . . . How I welcome my grim
fellow, and walk arm in arm with him ! . . . I
love him, he is so flexible, and yields to me as
the air to my body. I leap and dance in his
midst, and play with his beard till he smiles."
Finally, here is this rhapsody from the Journal:[1] " The luxury of wisdom ! the luxury of
virtue ! Are there any intemperate in these
things?" " He left all for the sake of certain

[1] *Journal*, II, 269.

virtuous self-indulgences," says Stevenson. He never gave up any vital part of himself from respect for universal law. He gave up only what he believed he did not need. " It is the greatest of all advantages to enjoy no advantage at all," he wrote.[1] He was what Sir Thomas Browne said Diogenes was, "more ambitious in refusing all Honours, than Alexander was in rejecting none." He made no renouncements outright; what renouncements he seems to have made he made only after he had gained his whole will and got his own way. He who wept at twenty to stay in Concord affected thereafter to scorn locality. He who evaded the crisis in which most youths choose professions was thereafter a loud despiser of professions "on principle." He rejected " the shocking and passionate," [2] not because he had outgrown them, but because he was without certain passions. The Stoic ideal is indifference to things we cannot command. Thoreau said, " I do not think much of the actual;" " Whatever actually happens to a man is wonderfully trivial and insignificant." [3] But he was far from indifferent to a number of things — his home, his freedom, his sphericity, his books, his boat, his Journal. If his Journal one day had burned, he would no doubt have jerked the long beard of Necessity in something like anger.

[1] *Journal*, ix, 160.   [2] *Ibid.*, ii, 3.   [3] *Ibid.*, ii, 43, 44.

IV

THE SPECIFIC

THOREAU is much more than an expansive bore. As all the greater transcendentalists had for saving remnants native qualities more vital and permanent than their rhapsodic and their German ingredients, — Carlyle his humor and his seer's powers and Emerson his flashing intellect, — so Thoreau has one natural gift which joins him to the ordinary world and saves him to posterity. That is his genius for the specific, his concreteness of character and vision. This genius is important both in his personality and in his authorship.

Thoreau is significant to culture in great measure because his personality is definite and unmistakable — "as free and erect a mind as any I have ever met," wrote Emerson in his Journal after first meeting Thoreau. There is a stanch and crackling integrity about the man which holds him, even at the moment of his most expansive departure, safe above the Romantic stupor of self-contemplation and self-absorption; when one reads this passage in a letter of 1854, one need not fear for Thoreau's self-possession : "I left the village and paddled up the river.

. . . I was smoothed with an infinite stillness.
I got the world, as it were, by the nape of the
neck, and held it under in the tide of its own
events, till it was drowned, and then I let it go
down-stream like a dead dog." If Thoreau is a
Buddhist he is a vigorous and a sprightly Buddhist. " The intellect is a cleaver; it discerns
and rifts its way into the secret of things," wrote
Thoreau in "Walden." There is a thrust, an as-
siduous, workmanlike quality in Thoreau's mental operations which marks him as distinct from
his fellows. Thoreau spoke always as a person, never as a mere metaphysician. Coleridge's
essay " On Sensibility " in the " Aids to Reflection " amounts almost to an epitome of Thoreau's thinking; but to no more than an epitome.

Thoreau's reaction to his friends and to society
is as sharp as any that is recorded. No other
naturalist has been so malicious; no other transcendentalist has been so fastidious. He draws
his personal circle very distinctly, to make sure
that it is seen. He is very positive; a college
essay begins, " The order of things should be re-
versed." He can be very disturbing as well, as
Stevenson sets forth in a clear paragraph : " His
system of personal economics . . . is based on one
or two ideas which, I believe, come naturally to all
thoughtful youths, and are only pounded out of
them by city uncles. Indeed, something essen-

tially youthful distinguishes all Thoreau's knock-
down blows at current opinion. Like the posers
of a child, they leave the orthodox in a kind of
speechless agony. These know the thing is non-
sense. They are sure there must be an answer, yet
somehow cannot find it. .... He attacks the subject
in a new dialect where there are no catchwords
ready made for the defender." Even after the
catchword is brought forth and the paradox is ex-
posed, he defeats still by a cool twinkling in the
eye which cannot be startled away. This passage
from " Life Without Principle " best exemplifies
what Stevenson was describing: " A strange age
of the world this, when empires, kingdoms, and
republics come a-begging to a private man's
door, and utter their complaints at his elbow! I
cannot take up a newspaper but I find that some
wretched government or other, hard pushed and
on its last legs, is interceding with me, the reader,
to vote for it, — more importunate than an Italian
beggar." When his expansion is hindered, he
strikes back very decisively. He knew his expansion was good; said so with a flash of the
eye; struck fire when challenged.

" For pure, nonsensical abstractions he had
no taste," thought Channing. He is interesting
to-day only in those respects in which he broke
out of the thick mystic cloud which enveloped
New England — broke out to breathe pure air

with George Herbert or Homer or Persius or
Confucius or the crab-apple tree. He could be
concise even in his mysticism — if that is not a
paradox. He has many unfledged, thick passages in the Journal, but they are not the best
of Thoreau, and need not be kept. It is vastly
to his credit that he selected the best of the
Journal, the most sensible, the most intelligible,
the most definite, for publication in " Walden "
and the " Week." For it is only when he is
definite, when, for example, he is telling what is
silent rather than preaching about Silence, that
he is valuable. He applied what others preached,
illustrated what others asserted, sought to make
sphericity lovely in the eyes of all men. " My
thought is a part of the meaning of the world,
and hence I use a part of the world as a symbol
to express my thought," he wrote.[1] He swore,
" Antæus-like," to " be not long absent from the
ground." It was by putting sphericity into figures, into terms of human economics, in " Walden," that he became a classic.

Thoreau is a specific Emerson. " The Service "
is " Circles " measured and cooled and visual-
ized — even brought home to earth in " the ele-
phant's rolling gait " and the " huge sphere
drawn along the streets." The lilt, airiness,
spontaneity of Emerson are sacrificed in Thoreau

[1] *Journal*, ɪv, 410.

for a more deliberate method; but that deliberation is worth something in itself. Emerson himself expounds its virtues: " In reading Henry Thoreau's journal I am very sensible of the vigor of his constitution. That oaken strength which I noted whenever he walked or worked or surveyed wood-lots, the same unhesitating hand with which a field-laborer accosts a piece of work which I should shun as a waste of strength, Henry shows in his literary strength. He has muscle, and ventures on and performs feats which I am forced to decline. In reading him I find the same thoughts, the same spirit that is in me, but he takes a step beyond and illustrates by excellent images that which I should have conveyed in a sleepy generalization. 'T is as if I went into a gymnasium and saw youths leap and climb and swing with a force unapproachable, though their feats are only continuations of my initial grapplings and jumps." [1] Thoreau is not satisfied with sleepy generalizations, but is passionate after what seems to him reality. He never lets himself forget that it is genuine experience he is seeking. " It is not easy to write in a journal what interests us at any time, because to write it is not what interests us," he wrote. Emerson had said, " There

[1] Emerson's Journal, quoted in E. W. Emerson, *Emerson in Concord* (1890), p. 113.

is no pure Transcendentalist "; Thoreau wished
to see what pure transcendentalism was, and
went to Walden. Emerson stands and guesses,
Thoreau goes and finds. Thoreau literally put
his whole life into his books. Emerson wishes
to talk mainly about tendencies and about expansive strivings, as in " Circles "; Thoreau
wishes to "drive life into a corner " and report
what he sees. He marked off a real circle of
individual rights. That he deceived himself is
not relevant here.

Thoreau was born an observer, and was not
ashamed of his gift. At twenty he praises Goethe
in the Journal because " he is generally satisfied
with giving an exact description of objects as
they appear to him." In a college essay he commended the " appetite for visible images " mani-
fested by Greek and Italian poets, and thought
the Northern poets rather inclined to a " fond-
ness for the dark and mysterious," a " neglect of
the material." Thoreau's " steps were winged with
the most eager expectation " ; he craved the sight
and feel of facts. A keen and single-minded
critic, he could see far into the more ordinary
human motives. His observations of people are
not profound, perhaps because they are few; his
metaphysical steed ran too fast, in the main, for
him to dare to glance aside at faces in the world.
But he did observe bodies and gaits and eccen-

tricities shrewdly now and then, as in "Cape Cod," where he is like Dickens, or in "Walden," in John Field's cottage. He was extraordinarily sensitive, like Stevenson himself, to the subtler of the superficial relations, as some passages can demonstrate : —

"There is a proper and only right way to enter a city, as well as to make advances to a strange person ; neither will allow of the least forwardness nor bustle. A sensitive person can hardly elbow his way boldly, laughing and talking, into a strange town, without experiencing some twinges of conscience, as when he has treated a stranger with too much familiarity." [1]

"It is a very true and expressive phrase, 'He looked daggers at me.' . . . It is wonderful how we get about the streets without being wounded by these delicate and glancing weapons, a man can so nimbly whip out his rapier, or without being noticed carry it unsheathed. Yet after all, it is rare that one gets seriously looked at." [2]

"With him [the lock-keeper at Middlesex] we had a just and equal encounter of the eyes, as between two honest men. The movements of the eyes express the perpetual and unconscious courtesy of the parties. It is said that a rogue does not look you in the face, neither does an

[1] *Journal*, i, 47.   [2] *Week*.

honest man look at you as if he had his reputa-
tion to establish. I have seen some who did not
know when to turn aside their eyes in meeting yours. A truly confident and magnanimous
spirit is wiser than to contend for the mastery in
such encounters. Serpents alone conquer by the
steadiness of their gaze. My friend looks me in
the face and sees me, that is all." [1]

It would be pleasant to hear more of Thoreau's
"Uncle Charles" Dunbar. A half-dozen paragraphs scattered through the Journal uncover in
Thoreau a gift for hitting off character which it
seems too bad was never improved.

September, 1850 : "Charles grew up to be a
remarkably eccentric man. He was of large frame,
athletic, and celebrated for his feats of strength.
His lungs were proportionally strong. There was
a man who heard him named once, and asked if
it was the same Charles Dunbar whom he remembered when he was a little boy walking on
the coast of Maine. A man came down to the
shore and hailed a vessel that was sailing by.
He should never forget that man's name."

April 3, 1856 : "Uncle Charles used to say that
he had n't a single tooth in his head. The fact was
they were all double, and I have heard that he lost
about all of them by the time he was twenty-one.
Ever since I knew him he could swallow his nose."

[1] *Week.*

March 11, 1859: " E. Hosmer says that a man told him that he had seen my uncle Charles take a twelve-foot ladder, set it up straight, and then run up and down the other side, kicking it from behind him as he went down."

January 15, 1853: " Saw near L——'s, the 12th, a shrike. He told me about seeing Uncle Charles once, come to Barrett's mill with logs, leap over the yoke that drew them and back again. It amused the boys."

January 1, 1853: " After talking with Uncle Charles the other night about the worthies of this country, Webster and the rest, as usual, considering who were geniuses and who were not, I showed him up to bed, and when I had got into bed myself, I heard his chamber door opened, after eleven o'clock, and he called out, in an earnest, stentorian voice, loud enough to wake the whole house, ' Henry! was John Quincy Adams a genius?' ' No, I think not,' was my reply. ' Well, I did n't think he was,' answered he."

Thoreau's genius for the specific is to be seen working on the largest scale in his assembling of isolated passages from various years of the Journal into such organic units as " Walden," the " Week," and " Cape Cod." Few readers realize that " Walden," for instance, is made up out of as many as sixteen years of the Journal

(1838–54). It is scarcely too generous to credit
him here with some measure of creative genius
— of which it has been asserted he has "not a
spark."[1] "He was probably reminded by his
delicate critical perception that the true business
of literature is with narrative," says Stevenson,
whose hobby can be forgiven for the once.
"Truth, even in literature, must be clothed with
flesh and blood, or it cannot tell its whole story
to the reader." Thoreau does have unquestion-
ably the story-teller's knack. He thought Æsop
would be intolerable if his morals only were
printed.[2] He understood that expectation is the
secret of the charm in romance, and has not a
few stealthy, intense fragments of narrative in

[1] This genius can best be appreciated by one who consults
the edition of *Walden* printed by the Bibliophile Society of
Boston, wherein Thoreau's original arrangement of the Journal pages out of which the present *Walden* was assembled is
followed faithfully by the editors, Mr. Harper and Mr. Sanborn. The differences between the earlier, less shapely
"book" and the classic of 1854 are many and great. It is
quite improbable that any other than Thoreau made the
changes. The publisher (who Mr. Harper intimates was responsible for the improvement) or any one could have removed
twelve thousand words easily enough; but it is scarcely thinkable that Thoreau, who was always jealous of his text, would
have entrusted the task of abridgment and unification to another; it is almost certain that no other than his own skillful
hand was the manipulator; the hand, whose ever it was,
touched so many parts of the manuscript that "it was necessary to make changes in nearly three hundred pages."

[2] *Journal*, III, 240.

his Journal. He understood, too, that people
read pictures, that the writer must seem to speak
out of somewhere, must seem to live perpetually
in such an atmosphere or even in such a locality
as only his art knows how to select and arrest
from the perplexing disorder of passing life. He
knew how to dress himself in a cloak of wistful
expectancy ; and he knew how to wrap the localities he was describing in "atmospheres," knew
how to make the spirit of the ponds and the
clearings permeate " Walden," the spirit of the
lazy river the " Week," the spirit of the omi-
nous sea "Cape Cod," and the spirit of the tall
forest the " Maine Woods." He believed in the
milieu.

His talent for organization is even more than
this ; it contains elements of the dramatic. The
paragraphs on "Uncle Charles" show an apti-
tude for " humours," and chapters in "Cape Cod"
have been likened to Dickens. Thoreau confesses
to that temperamental dualism which creators
of " humours " are likely to experience, and which
forced Daudet almost against his will, as he
stood by his mother's coffin, to set to grouping
the surroundings (including himself) into a tab-
leau suitable to fiction. " I . . . am sensible of a
certain doubleness by which I can stand as remote
from myself as from another," Thoreau wrote.[1]

[1] *Journal*, IV, 291.

He could group his impressions and experiences, and frame his picture with facts, like a playwright — or an *encadreur*. He had a predilection for some kind of unity; an island pleased his imagination because it was " integral " and " continent." The vicinity of Walden Pond, the beach at Cape Cod, the seven-day stretch of the Merrimac and Concord Rivers, are geographical or at least psychological units. The reader is never without a feeling of satisfaction, as of being certain of his location and his directions. The beanfield, the village, the ponds, the woods are as important in " Walden " perhaps as the ideas there upon economy or upon Homer. The railroad and the train crew are most skillfully employed as points of reference — as foils for ideas — as guaranties of reality. And when Thoreau says he lay for a long time at the edge of a hole in the ice and mooned at the uneven floor of the pond, his readers see him in his proper place upon a stage; and they never wish themselves out of the audience and looking over his shoulder. This illusion of place is most admirably achieved in " Walden " of all Thoreau's works; Thoreau is everywhere effective in proportion as he deals in this illusion. It would be unjust to him to say that it is accidental in " Walden." He was as conscious of a dramatic mission there as he was of a spiritual mission in " The Service."

Thoreau's genius for the specific was of the first importance in his writing, where he strove to precipitate the vapor of a cloudy philosophy in fixed, crystal drops, and where his most enduring excellence surely lies; it is of the first importance now to any one who would study his theory and practice of composition.

It is hardly too much to say that for Thoreau, even in the most literal sense, writing meant living. "I think Thoreau had always looked forward to authorship as his work in life," said Emerson. Channing thought that "no matter where he might have lived, or in what circumstance, he would have been a writer; he was made for this by all his tendencies of mind and temperament"; and records that "it was a saying of his that he had lived and written as if to live forty years longer; his work was laid out for a long life." [1]

Such testimony establishes his passion. More testimony establishes his good faith. If he had a passion for writing, and so for living, he had also a passion for writing perfectly and so for living completely. He wrote every day in his Journal for training; he composed prose while he walked; and always he devoted his powers to the written page, refusing to strive for any unusual effects

---

[1] Thoreau left, among other literary effects, eleven manuscript volumes, or about three thousand pages, filled laboriously with notes on the Indians, of whom it is known he intended to write an elaborate study.

in his lecturing. He understood that "nothing
goes by luck in composition," and took to heart
Carlyle's condemnation of Novalis for not "trou-
bling to express his truth with any laborious
accuracy" for "want of rapid energy . . . and
. . . the emphasis and resolute force of a man."
He hated "palaver" in style, and said he did
manual labor in order to outgrow it. "It is
vain to try to write unless you feel strong in the
knees," said Thoreau.

Thoreau subscribed to conciseness and indi-
viduality in his writing as elsewhere. In 1851
he was reminding himself by a footnote in the
Journal, —

" My faults are : —
    Paradoxes, — saying just the opposite, — a
        style which may be imitated.
    Ingenious.
    Using current phrases and maxims, when I
        should speak for myself.
    Want of conciseness."

He envied the Greeks because they could "express themselves with more facility than we in
distinct and lively images." He hated "wooden
and lifeless" words, with "paralysis in their
tails," as he hated gossip. He was a good work-
man, filing rather more finely than Emerson took
the trouble to file. " Every sentence is the result

of a long probation," he said, and "should read as if its author, had he held a plough instead of a pen, could have drawn a furrow deep and straight to the end." "The prose writer has conquered like a Roman, and settled colonies," it seemed to him. He omitted no practicable measures for perfecting his equipment. "Henry Thoreau says he values only the man who goes directly to his needs; who, wanting wood, goes to the woods and brings it home," said Channing. He disciplined himself by studying Herbert and Quarles, and by translating two dramas of Æschylus and selections from Homer, Anacreon, and Pindar; he aped the styles of a dozen prose-masters. The most remarkable product of his mimicry is the last paragraph of the chapter called "The Pond in Winter" in "Walden," which moves with many a token of the gait of Sir Thomas Browne. All in all, Thoreau, if not radiant, writes so satisfactorily that the critic is tempted (and his earlier critics did not in fact resist the temptation) to do nothing but fill his space with quotations; for Thoreau can take the matter in hand away from the bungling expositor and dispatch it in a phrase or paragraph that calls for no amendment.

It is not difficult to decide to what school of literary theorists Thoreau belongs. He was a nineteenth-century euphuist of the stamp of Flau-

bert, Stevenson, and Pater ; he travailed to catch
consciousness itself in the trap of the specific;
he wished to express " himself." " Men are constantly dinging in my ears their fair theories and
plausible solutions of the universe, but ever there
is no help, and I return again to my shoreless,
islandless ocean, and fathom unceasingly for a
bottom that will hold an anchor." [1] He believed
that if he could come squarely upon his self, and
could describe that self exactly, he would be an-
chored for once and all. His whole literary quest
was a quest for a charm by which he could trans-
fer the facts of consciousness — to him as to many
men of letters in the nineteenth century the only
reality — to the printed page. He watched his
" moods . . . as narrowly as a cat does a mouse,"
he said. " He had as touchstone for authors their
degree of ability to deal with supersensual facts
and feeling with scientific precision and dignity,"
an acquaintance wrote. For him " thought "
meant " impression," and " impression " meant
" reality." He considered that he should have
come nearest reality when he had " kinked and
knotted " his impressions into " something hard
and significant, which you could swallow like a
diamond, without digesting." [2] He wished his
" life " to go into his books, and is alarmed in
1840 [3] when he considers " how little I am *actu-*

[1] *Journal,* i, 54.   [2] *Ibid.,* ii, 419.   [3] *Ibid.,* i, 143.

ally concerned about the things I write in my journal." He wished his books to present an absolutely new front of life, a new kind of reality — his own life, and his own " reality." " If you can write what you will never read, you have done rare things," he said in the " Week." He was zealous in the cause of expressing particular — and so for him the only genuine — impressions ; he has much to say to that man who can see no difference between one green field and another. He comes nearest, perhaps, to convincing his readers of what they should be steadfastly reluctant to believe — that there is anything new under the sun — in such a passage as this impeccable one from the " Maine Woods " : " Once, when Joe [the Indian guide] had called again, and we were listening for moose, we heard, come faintly echoing, or creeping from afar, through the moss-clad aisles, a dull, dry, rushing sound with a solid core to it, yet as if half-smothered under the grasp of the luxuriant and fungus-like forest, like the shutting of a door in some distant entry of the damp and shaggy wilderness. If we had not been there, no mortal had heard it. When we asked Joe in a whisper what it was, he answered, ' Tree fall.' "

Thoreau is definitely related to the nineteenth-century prose " school of the particular," perhaps in the capacity of pioneer, through his influence upon Stevenson. There is no question that Stevenson took much from Thoreau. Both began by imitating. The very first sentence of "The Service" would have done, as far as tone is concerned, for the first sentence of "Æs Triplex." The "Week" reminds one of the "Inland Voyage" in the first paragraph and on almost every page thereafter. The trick of defining one impression by bringing another impression smartly alongside — "it is as if the beasts spoke"[1] — Stevenson could have learned in the pages of Thoreau. Had Stevenson not been fascinated by the man himself, his judgments upon him could not have been as trenchant and subtle as they were; he told some one in an enthusiastic moment that he supposed he had never written ten words after he had once read Thoreau which would not recall him.

Thoreau, isolated in America, his wits straying through the endless and utterly formless reaches of a transcendental Journal, did not end his literary career as happily as Flaubert and Stevenson, writers of finished stories, and Pater, writer of finished essays, ended theirs. Fatally committed to sphericity, always, unfortunately, conscious of "eternity and space gambolling familiarly through my depths,"[2] he had not the means of improving and disciplining his native

[1] Thoreau on Whitman.   [2] *Journal*, I, 54.

genius for the specific which Pater had in his
intellectual ideal of beauty and his better understanding of the Greek feeling that the half yields
greater satisfaction to the spirit than the whole.
So that while the Greeks could " prune his orations and point his pen," and do somewhat to
give him " bottom, endurance, wind,"[1] they
never gave Thoreau to understand that scrutiny
of consciousness itself needs scrutiny. By 1850
he had forgotten to translate from the Greek,
had forgotten to discipline his Journal prose by
exercising in verse, and had fallen into the
grasp of as relentless a demon of romantic composition as is anywhere to be seen in literature.
" His literary art," says Burroughs, " was to let
fly with a kind of quick inspiration." He tells
himself in the Journal that the theme seeks him,
not he it ; that he " fears no intemperance," but
is prepared to " drain the cup of inspiration to
its last dregs " ; that he is ambitious to " take as
many bounds in a day as possible." He did take
some very extravagant bounds in his Journal,
believing implicitly that his natural mind was
inexhaustible, welcoming any impression that
was sharp and vivid, " improving every op-
portunity to express himself as if it were the
last," making the most of every fancy lest if rejected it prove to have been important, piling

[1] Emerson, *English Traits.*

up examples and talking all around a subject in hopes of getting to it "naturally." In proportion as he grew desperate in his pursuit of the one germ at last which when swallowed would expand him indefinitely, he grew less effectual in his self-expression. The style and the self, whenever they dissipated, dissipated together. Perhaps a commission from the demon to labor for years on a work like "Marius the Epicurean" was what he, the writer, stood in need of, he the diamond disintegrating in his brave vacuum on the rock-bound coast of New England.

V

READING

" WE confess," wrote Lowell in his first essay on Thoreau, "that there is a certain charm for us even about a fool who has read myriads of books. There is an undefinable atmosphere around him as of distant lands around a great traveller, and of distant years around very old men." Lowell, who is far from insinuating that Thoreau is a fool, here puts the student on the track of what is soundest and most engaging in Thoreau — his love and use of books. His genius for the specific did not fail him here but made of him (not to speak of the writer in him which it distinguished) a reader whose every remark rings true and inviting.

Thoreau is a literary epicure of a superior order. He has neither the dissolute fastidiousness of a Sylvestre Bonnard nor the all-devouring hunger of an Emerson. He does not go mad over a quoted delicacy or a rare title, and he does not read ubiquitously for the sensation of inspiration. But he has that " undefinable atmosphere around him " which lies around any man who seems to have all the time in the world to do what he pleases — in Thoreau's case the man who has all the time in the world to read and reread his favorite books. And since it is in his reading that Thoreau has most control of himself, his example is not bad. It is the chapter on " Reading " in " Walden," with its reminder that the language of the classics is dead only to the degenerate, and its assertion that " books must be read as deliberately and reservedly as they were written " which marks him as a scholar and which distinguishes him from some of his less self-contained contemporaries.

Perhaps his distinction as a writer and as a personality is to be ascribed to the fact that he studied only what was best in college, that he settled down to the luxurious, wonderful task of reading the older English poets through and did not always bother to gulp down the last piece of mystic bait from Germany or England. The charm and even value of his work may prove eventually to lie where the charm of his favorite Persius lies, in its bookishness. Thoreau knew pretty definitely from the beginning what he wanted to read, and he was able to keep himself within the wholesome limits which his instinct and conscience set. He has not the transcendental pride in catholicity of reading but chooses his fields like a self-reliant scholar.[1]

[1] Six fly-leaves in the back of Thoreau's copy of the *Traveller's Guide through the United States* (1838), a little book car-

There is a rare workmanlike air about Thoreau's handling of books. When he reports

ried by him on one or more of his excursions, and now in the possession of Mr. George S. Hellman, are covered with the following pencil-notes, written in apparent hurry and without comment: —

    14th   Castine to Belfast by packet Capt. Skinner
    15th   Belfast to Bath
    16th   Wednesday, to Portland
    17 — to Boston — Concord

Campbell's Poems
Sally Russell's Letters
La Nouvelle Héloise.
Akenside
Emile

Chefs D'Œuvre de Corneille.

Johnson's Lives of the Poets.

Goethe

Lettres Choisies de Mme De Sevigne et De Maintenon.
Am. Lib. Use. Knowl.
  Universal History

Mechanics, Pneumatics, etc.

Pilgrim's Progress

Œuvres Complètes De Platon 12 vols.

Sir Th. Browne's Works 4 vols.

Horace Walpole Private Correspondence

Studies of Nature

Leighton

Johnson
Donne's Devotions.
Seneca's Morals
Fielding's Proverbs
Philip Van Artevelde
Lardner's Cyc. Astronomy & Study of Nat. Phil.

Montaigne

Mrs. Somerville
Wotton

his reading it is from isolation, and is as if a
cabinet-maker stepped out of his shop to exhibit a pet piece of his own making. When
one hears that he read Chalmers's "Poets"
through, one sees him sitting alone in rare quiet,
fondling his book much as a carpenter squints
along a smoothed board, or a sailor trims his
yarn on a pile of canvas. He read as systemati-
cally as his means allowed in such fields as the
older English poets, the seventeenth century, the
classics, and the Oriental Scriptures, always
in this workmanlike fashion.   Intensely serious,

De Stael's Germany
Ben Johnson
Beaumont and Fletcher
Moliere
St. Augustine
Malte Brun
Anecdotes of Eminent Persons
Lib. Use. Knowl. Some vols.

Gibbon

Hume

Lord Bacon

Percy Anecdotes

Burton

Bakewell's Geology
Burke
Clarendon
Blackwood
Dr. Byrom's Misc. Poems. 2 v.
Wither's Britain's Remembrancer
Norris
Henry More
Quarles
Crashaw's Steps to the Temple
Wilmott's Lives of the Sacred Poets.

sedulously intent on self-improvement, he selected with precision and read for strength. He
had a quick and true eye for excellence. "He
would pass by many delicate rhythms," says
Emerson, "but he would detect every live stanza
or line in a volume, and knew very well where
to find an equal poetic charm in prose." One
would like to have seen his collection of "extracts from the noblest poetry."

An understanding of this bent for refining the
best from books — crystal sentences, precious
lines, and fine flavors — will take the student
farthest along the way of his reading, and do
most to explain why he tarried here, why he
never left there, why he passed this field by, why
he set up an idol in that place.

An understanding of his philosophical position,
which was almost identical with Emerson's, will
not be half so useful a tool as this very keen one of
his literary tact. Thus a very satisfactory foundation for the whole of his thinking might be built
out of such passages in the four volumes of the
"Dial" as this (from an essay in the second number, "The Art of Life — The Scholar's Call-
ing"[1]): "Life is an art. When we consider what
life may be to all, and what it is to most, we shall
see how little this art is yet understood. . . . The
work of life, so far as the individual is concerned,

[1] *Dial*, I, 175.

and that to which the scholar is particularly called, is *self-culture*, — the perfect unfolding of our individual nature. . . . The business of self-culture admits of no compromise. Either it must be made a distinct aim, or wholly abandoned. 'I respect the man,' says Goethe, 'who knows distinctly what he wishes.' . . . In all things the times are marked by a want of steady aim and patient industry. . . . The young man launches into life with no definite course in view. . . . The sure satisfaction which accompanies the consciousness of progress in the true direction towards the stature of a perfect man. Let him who would build . . . consider well the cost. . . . Much . . . he will have to renounce. . . . No emoluments must seduce him from the rigor of his devotion. No engagements beyond the merest necessities of life must interfere with his pursuit. A meagre economy must be his income. . . . The rusty coat must be his badge. Obscurity must be his distinction. . . . The business of society is not . . . the highest culture, but the greatest comfort. . . . On all hands man's existence is converted into a preparation for existence. We do not properly live in these days. . . . We cannot get to ourselves. . . . Consciousness stops half way. O! for some moral Alaric, who should sweep away all that has been in this kind. . . . The highest life is the life of the mind, the enjoyment of thought. Between this life and any point of outward existence, there is never but one step, and that step is an act of the will. The business of self-culture is to live now, to live in the present, to live in the highest. . . . This habit of living for effect [is] utterly incompatible with wholesome effort and an earnest mind. No heroic character, no depth of feeling, or clearness of insight can ever come of such a life. All that is best in human attainments springs from retirement. . . . In retirement we first become acquainted with ourselves, our means, and ends. Whatever selfishness there may seem to be in such a discipline as this, exists only in appearance. . . . In self-culture lies the ground and condition of all culture. . . . The silent influence of example . . . is the true reformer. . . . Society are more benefited by one sincere life, by seeing how one man has helped himself, than by all the projects that human policy has devised for their salvation. . . . All truth must be lived before it can be adequately known or taught. . . . The scholar has his function . . . he must be a radical in speculation, an ascetic in devotion, a cynic in independence, an anchorite in his habits, a perfectionist in discipline. Secluded from without, and nourished from within. . . . It is to such men that we must look for the long expected literature of this nation. . . . We have no practical poets, — no epic lives." Philosophi-

cally considered, Thoreau has little more to say
than the voluble writers of the " Dial " had to say.
But he is more than a philosopher ; and why the
artist in him could step, half-Phœnix and half-
Chanticleer, clear-voiced and clean-limbed out of
the swaddling-clothes of the Orphic "Dial,"
only his genius can explain.

Thoreau was most drawn to and was most dur-
ably nourished by three literary springs — the
Oriental Scriptures, the classics, and the older
English poets. Outside of these (if the English
Bible, and Emerson, whose books he "rarely
looked at," [1] and Carlyle, whose style he admired
but could not possibly imitate, are excepted) it is
seldom necessary to go for literary influences. He
disliked German metaphysics and the involved
German language. Indeed, it is impossible for one
who appreciates the quiet, clear, spare, hard Gaul
and Scot in him to link him for any reason with
the German metaphysicians; just as it is impossible not to link with them Coleridge when he was
steeped in opium and thick mystic eloquence, or
Carlyle when he played the rôle of coffee-drinking,
sulphurous mystic, hounded by his own energy.
" He had no favorite among the French or Germans," it was said.   One must stick to the solitary
" heroic writers of antiquity," and to "those
books which circulate round the world, whose

[1] *Journal*, iii, 134.

sentences were first written on bark, and are now
merely copied from time to time onto linen paper,"
for "sources" of Thoreau.

"We read the Orientals, but remain Occidental. The fewest men receive anything from
their studies," said Emerson. Thoreau remained
as Occidental as any man could be; he took from
his Oriental reading merely what he was pleased to
clip away; and it was always he, Thoreau, who
took it. So that while he "had the best library
of Oriental books in the country," and was as de-
lighted over Cholmondeley's gift as he might have
been at "the birth of a child," the total influence
of Oriental philosophy upon Thoreau was neither
broad nor profound. He neither embraced it
lightly as a cloistral dream, nor sounded it stu-
diously for its deepest meaning. He cannot be said
to have understood the true significance of the
Oriental position, with its stern dualism, its difficult discipline (which in the "Week" he called
"moral drudgery"), its pessimism and its resig-
nation. He, like Emerson and the other transcendentalists, was content to declare jauntily that
"the Buddhist is a transcendentalist," or to ape
the Zoroastrian hilltop worship on some Concord
eminence, and do little more.

Thoreau took figures and sentences, not ideas,
from his Oriental reading. It was the sentences
that stayed on his mind, and which he says he

annoyed the neighbors with repeating. "One wise sentence is worth the State of Massachusetts many times over," was his judgment. If Emerson intellectualized the Oriental Scriptures, Thoreau used whatever sayings in them could crisply advise him what to do or neatly and with an air of finality justify what he did. There is something youthful and delightful about the liberties this crisp, deft man takes with the heavy-tongued Orientals. It is the liberty which a curious and earnest youth, ambitious to know old and great things, disliking the "shocking and passionate," perhaps deceived by vague mystery and high talk but craving confidence and bottom, takes with any wisdom that is ripe and of long standing.

One thing more important than sentences Thoreau took from the Orientals; and that was no such thing as the consciousness of standing "on the meeting of two eternities, the past and future, which is precisely the present moment," but something more sincere and vital. Thoreau is probably most interesting for his attitude on practical questions concerning the personal relations. Thoreau's native hatred of philanthropy must have been materially reinforced by contact with what Orientalists to-day hold up to the humanitarian West as the "true spirit of charity," the Oriental doctrine of cold benevolence and separation in friendship. He must have relished this sen-

tence which he edited for the "Dial" in 1843 : [1]
"Be silent, for I swear by Allah, it were equal
to the torments of hell to enter into Paradise
through the interest of a neighbor."

Thoreau was somewhat better fitted to understand and appropriate the Greek spirit than he
was the Oriental spirit. Brought up among persons who knew the value of Greek, and writing
in a company (Parker, Miss Fuller, Alcott)
which was extraordinarily proficient in the Greek
language, Thoreau could not but take notice of
the claims of classical literature upon the modern
attention. That he did so with greater zest and
to better advantage than his fellows is significant. It is told that he read "Latin as readily as
English," and "Greek without difficulty." [2] He
was a more careful scholar, in this as in other
fields, than Emerson. Thoreau "never had a
good word to say for Plato" — possibly because
he distrusted the Neo-Platonism of Emerson ;
but he "read all the Greek poets in the original." [3]

It seems too much to say what a recent writer
has said, that "he was almost a transplanted
Greek." He was no Greek at all in respect of
temper — unless, indeed, Greek life was a life of
eccentricity and the Greek spirit was the spirit

[1] *Dial*, iv, 404.
[2] F. B. Sanborn, *Personality of Thoreau*, p. 36.   [3] *Ibid.*

of exaggeration. Thoreau announced what is almost a gospel of exaggeration: "I desire to speak somewhere without bounds; for I am convinced that I cannot exaggerate enough even to lay the foundation of a true expression." He did not begin to have the balance of temper which warns that important truth can scarcely be arrived at by assertion or founded on exaggeration. In general, he confessed in the "Week," he found Greece and Rome "tame"; though he praised Homer like a wild boy — crediting him with absolute realism and perfect naturalness, a magic power to describe the morning itself rather than an impression of it, and so on. He was relished in his day, it is said, as being "the only man who thoroughly loved both Nature and Greek." He spoke without bounds concerning Greece, and he spoke without bounds concerning Nature; disclosing, perhaps, that he knew the human bearings of neither any too well.

Yet Greece furnished Thoreau a very effective means for artistic discipline in the way of a standard outside of New England and himself. Emerson had said in the "Dial" that the classics gave "the purest pleasure accessible to human nature." Thoreau assured the readers of "Walden" that "the student may read Homer or Æschylus in the Greek without danger of dissipation or luxuriousness, for it implies that he in some measure emulate their heroes, and consecrate morning hours to their pages." Besides, Greece was favored by the gods with the gift of perfection; "over Greece hangs the divine necessity, a mellow heaven of itself," he wrote in "The Service." There was sufficient exhortation in the "Dial" to "study their works and learn their methods." Emerson was only expressing a general transcendental conviction when he commended the study of the Greeks to the writer because they "prune his orations and point his pen." Thoreau's study of the Greek Anthology enabled him to write at least two pointed and excellent poems. One, "Mist," almost purely Greek and quite without fault, Cholmondeley considered Thoreau's best piece : —

> "Low-anchored cloud,
> Newfoundland air,
> Fountain-head and source of rivers,
> Dew-cloth, dream-drapery,
> And napkin spread by fays;
> Drifting meadow of the air,
> Where bloom the daisied banks and violets,
> And in whose fenny labyrinth
> The bittern booms and heron wades ;
> Spirit of lakes and seas and rivers,
> Bear only perfumes and the scent
> Of healing herbs to just men's fields."

The other, "Smoke," scarcely less Greek or more exceptionable, Emerson thought suggested Simon-

ides — " but is better than any poem of Simoni-
des ": —

> " Light-winged Smoke, Icarian bird,
>   Melting thy pinions in thy upward flight,
>   Lark without song, and messenger of dawn,
>   Circling above the hamlets as thy nest;
>   Or else, departing dream, and shadowy form
>   Of midnight vision, gathering up thy skirts;
>   By night star-veiling, and by day
>   Darkening the light and blotting out the sun;
>   Go thou my incense upward from this hearth,
>   And ask the gods to pardon this clear flame."

These and similar exercises furnished no such
discipline as Matthew Arnold sought in the
classics, and it can scarcely be said that any of
the American transcendentalists was diligent
and patient enough to reap the " high benefit of
clearly feeling and deeply enjoying the really excellent." Thoreau spoke of classical studies as
" composing "; but genuine composure was not a
transcendental virtue.

" If men read aright, methinks they would
never read anything but poems," runs a passage
in the " Week." Thoreau, who devoted his college days to working in the mine of old English
poetry, owes more to the styles and the tempera-
ments of the early poets than he owes to any other
group of writers. Hardly a page is not reminis-
cent of one of them. "Old Chaucer's breadth"
taught him that "there is no wisdom which can

take the place of humanity ";[1] and Chaucer's
clearness and raciness were by no means lost on
Thoreau's style. The subtle qualities of Daniel
were not lost on Thoreau. The admirable stanza
beginning the poem " To the Lady Margaret,
Countess of Cumberland ": —

> " He that of such a height hath built his mind,
>   And rear'd the dwelling of his thoughts so strong,
>   As neither fear nor hope can shake the frame
>   Of his resolvèd powers; nor all the wind
>   Of vanity or malice pierce to wrong
>   His settled peace, or to disturb the same;
>   What a fair seat hath he, from whence he may
>   The boundless wastes and wilds of man survey ! " —

might have been a text for an essay ; he did
quote time and again the famous lines from the
same poem, —

> " Unless above himself he can
> Erect himself, how poor a thing is man."

He thought Daniel deserved praise " for his
moderation," and said, " We can well believe
that he was a retired scholar, who would keep
himself shut up in his house two whole months
together." He thought both Donne and Daniel
had " strong sense," and respected the former
because he had the " patience of a day laborer."[2]
He admired Drayton's vigor, independence, and
realism, and he commended old English tragedy

---

[1] *Journal*, I, 301.   [2] *Ibid.*, I, 467.

because "it says something," moves "toward
some conclusion," " has to do with things," is
" downright and manly," and because its writers
" come to the point and do not waste the time." [1]
He had not much patience with the romantic
criticism of Shakespeare, [2] believing that the
critics obscured his " chief characteristics of
reality and unaffected manliness." He quotes
often enough from Shakespeare; but he did not
reverence him as he reverenced Milton.

Thoreau's favorite and most important resort
in old English poetry was to the religious poets
of the seventeenth century — Donne, Vaughan,
Crashaw, Quarles, and Herbert. He was gen-
uinely akin to them in temperament, found
their themes congenial, and made the most of
their metrical example. They were much in
favor with the New England transcendentalists.
Emerson was devoted to Herbert from the beginning, and Alcott had only one contemporary
in his list of favorite poets: Wordsworth, Milton,
Donne, Vaughan, Crashaw, Herbert, Quarles,
and Cowley.

In the main Thoreau's affinity with these poets
was temperamental and spiritual; he admired
Quarles only for his metallic qualities of verse
and voice, and his eminently sturdy constitution.
He found in him " plenty of tough, crooked tim-

[1] *Journal*, i, 465.   [2] *Ibid.*, i, 466.

ber," and wrote in his Journal,[1] "Quarles is never weak or shallow, though coarse and untasteful. He presses able-bodied and strong-backed words into his service, which have a certain rustic fragrance and force, as if now first devoted to literature after having served sincere and stern uses . . . a right manly accent." In the main Thoreau was drawn by their sober introspection and intense concentration to the seventeenth-century religious poets, preferring them on this ground to the Elizabethans. Milton he read always, valuing him " above Shakespeare," and getting "Lycidas" by heart. In the others their more morbid and egoistic elements of eccentricity and nervous, crabbed intensity fascinated him. Their poetry was made pretty largely out of the nerves, and Thoreau was not without nerves. He repaired to them for the discipline of their form, but indulged himself in the vehemence of their sentiment. Like them, he could not finish a poem as bravely as he could begin it.

Thoreau probably felt the seventeenth century most through George Herbert, whose almost morbid sensitiveness to details, whose strained simplicity, whose tremulous purity, whose low-voiced passion combined with what Emerson described as his " hard mentality," his " grip and exactitude of mind," and his " mental materialism "

[1] *Journal,* I, 458–59.

to make Thoreau something, certainly, of what he was. Thoreau had very little to say explicitly about Herbert, just as he had little to say about Emerson, another prime influence in his life. Emerson and Herbert — at least the qualities of mind they represented — Thoreau took for granted. He could never weld a poem as heated and as pure as the best of Herbert; he was with difficulty sweet. But the signs of his vain strivings are many; and the Herbert in him never died. The youth who drew his breath in pain for every line of poetry he tried, did not outgrow that pain, however early he ceased trying to write poetry; he wrote nervous and excellent prose largely by virtue of it.

Thoreau seems to have been bent very early toward Herbert. The best poem from his early period, and one of the best of all his poems, " Sic Vita " (1837), is unmistakably like the Herbert of " Employment " and " Denial " and the rest in almost every technical feature : —

> " I am a parcel of vain strivings tied
>   By a chance bond together,
> Dangling this way and that, their links
>   Were made so loose and wide,
>   Methinks,
>   For milder weather.

> " A bunch of violets without their roots,
>   And sorrel intermixed,

Encircled by a wisp of straw
  Once coiled about their shoots,
      The law
  By which I 'm fixed.

" A nosegay which Time clutched from out
    Those fair Elysian fields,
  With weeds and broken stems, in haste,
    Doth make the rabble rout
        That waste
    The day he yields.

" And here I bloom for a short hour unseen,
    Drinking my juices up,
  With no root in the land
    To keep my branches green,
          But stand
    In a bare cup.

" Some tender buds were left upon my stem
    In mimicry of life,
  But ah ! the children will not know,
    Till time has withered them,
          The woe
    With which they 're rife.

" But now I see I was not plucked for naught,
    And after in life's vase
  Of glass set while I might survive,
    But by a kind hand brought
          Alive
    To a strange place.

" That stock thus thinned will soon redeem its
          hours,
    And by another year,

Such as God knows, with freer air,
More fruits and fairer flowers
Will bear,
While I droop here." [1]

---

[1] EMPLOYMENT

If as a flower doth spread and die,
   Thou wouldst extend me to some good,
Before I were by frost's extremity
         Nipt in the bud,

The sweetness and the praise were Thine,
   But the extension and the room,
Which in Thy garland I should fill, were mine
         At Thy great doom.

For as Thou dost impart Thy grace,
   The greater shall our glory be.
The measure of our joys is in this place,
         The stuff with Thee.

Let me not languish then, and spend
   A life as barren to Thy praise
As is the dust to which that life doth tend,
         But with delays.

All things are busy; only I
   Neither bring honey with the bees,
Nor flowers to make that, nor the husbandry
         To water these.

I am no link of Thy great chain,
   But all my company is a weed.
Lord, place me in Thy concert; give one strain
         To my poor reed.

DENIAL

When my devotions could not pierce
         Thy silent ears,

An inferior poem of the next year, called "Friendship" in the Journal,[1] continues the tradition : —

Then was my heart broken, as was my verse;
    My breast was full of fears
        And disorder.

My bent thoughts, like a brittle bow,
        Did fly asunder :
Each took his way; some would to pleasures go,
    Some to the wars and thunder
        Of alarms.

As good go anywhere they say,
        As to benumb
Both knees and heart in crying night and day,
    "Come, come, my God, O come!"
        But no hearing.

O that Thou shouldst give dust a tongue
        To cry to thee,
And then not hear it crying! All day long
    My heart was in my knee,
        But no hearing.

Therefore my soul lay out of sight,
        Untuned, unstrung :
My feeble spirit, unable to look right,
    Like a nipt blossom hung
        Discontented.

O cheer and tune my heartless breast,
        Defer no time;
That so Thy favors granting my request,
    They and my mind may chime,
        And mend my rhyme.

[1] *Journal*, i, 40–41.

"I think awhile of Love, and, while I think,
　　Love is to me a world,
　　Sole meat and sweetest drink,
　　And close connecting link
　　　'Tween heaven and earth.

"I only know it is, not how or why,
　　My greatest happiness;
　　However hard I try,
　　Not if I were to die,
　　　Can I explain.

"I fain would ask my friend how it can be,
　　But, when the time arrives,
　　Then Love is more lovely
　　Than anything to me,
　　　And so I 'm dumb."

. . . .

Hereafter the visible signs of Herbert in Thoreau fade; but the quiet, passionate conviction which was the mark of his early style is not extinguished by maturer sarcasm, nor even stung to death by wild-apple tang. Herbert could not enlist Thoreau in the enterprise of "making humility lovely in the eyes of all men"; but he could teach him in some measure his technique of living — how to feel, and how to write.

VI

POSITION

THOREAU'S permanent, best qualities — his sly and edged excellence, his leavening power — come into fuller recognition as his less essential qualities are subtracted and retreat. He is properly discounted only as his readers grow civilized and distrust the exposition of the elementary; he will come fully into his own when there is no one left who takes him literally and recommends his audacity as either profound or ultimate. The by-products of his living and his thinking — the excellences of the " Week " and " Walden," and whatever he prepared for print — are more essential than their central product, the extravagances of the Journal. His theory of life, so neatly conceived, so skillfully and variously expressed, so pointedly reinforced by reading and quotation, comes ultimately to seem futile and somewhat less than adequate; while the very neatness of conception, the very skill and variety and flavor of expression, the very quotations, endure. That Thoreau's main product was nothing, and his main effort vain, his own Journal best betrays. Emerson thought " he had exhausted all the capabilities of life in this world." The many

to p. 46

pages of the Journal which uncover his private sense of bewilderment and pain when friends disappeared and confess his growing impotence in expansion, are the flattest denial that Thoreau died with any such conviction in his heart.

Yet the Journal is also the best witness that it was indeed Thoreau's ambition to exhaust all the capabilities of life in this world. Better still, the Journal reveals why he had to fail. It is the Journal which gives the best clue to the character of Thoreau's thinking, which gives to understand that Thoreau's whole philosophical significance is involved in the fact that he thought in a vacuum.

It is very specifically that Thoreau says he inhabits a vacuum, and it is very adroitly that he defends his choice of habitation; it is perhaps in spite of himself that he proves better than almost any other theorizer the ultimate futility of all living in a vacuum. At any rate, his very clear remarks upon the subject, and his most relentless pursuit of its essence, make him a very satisfactory figure in which to observe its bearings and its consequences. Within his vacuum Thoreau was to become perfect with the least difficulty, was to be reborn into the Universe with the slightest travail. He was to be all that Man can be, at once and forever. He was to find Reality and keep it for a companion. By

taking thought he was to achieve absolute glory.
And all would be very easy. "The brave man
braves nothing," he boasted in "The Service."
" What a hero one can be without moving a finger !" "Not having anything to do, to do something." To be a real man — how extremely easy,
if only one has courage to slough real responsi-
bilities ! Intellectual perfection was quite within
reach. "One may have many thoughts and not
decide anything," decided Thoreau. He had only
to knock the bottom out of his consciousness to
know how unfathomably profound he was. He
had only to withdraw into a dark corner to witness how pure white was the flame of his thought.
Moral perfection was even a simpler matter *in
vacuo*. Emerson had thrown out the disconcert-
ing statement in " The Transcendentalist " that
" We have yet no man who has leaned entirely
upon his character." Thoreau could do that easily enough. All he needed to do was to "rise
above the necessity of virtue," so that his vices
would "necessarily trail behind," and to facilitate
the operation of the will by removing all the
occasions for exercising it. He could not but be
perfect when he was above having to be tested.
He could solve any problem in his vacuum absolutely to his satisfaction. He proposed, for instance, to

> " Find out heaven
> By not knowing hell."

Complete æsthetic and spiritual satisfaction also came easily in the vacuum. The humming of a telegraph-wire could supply the first; the second was inherent in a life of vacuous expansion. " Simplify, simplify ! " cried Thoreau like a Rousseau in " Walden." In his vacuum he simplified the meaning of exaltation of soul until it became equivalent to the sensation of expansion, equivalent to the reminder (from anywhere) " that there were higher, infinitely higher, planes of life which it behooved me never to forget." [1] That sensation and that reminder he demanded infinite room to indulge and hearken for. No other mortal could be near ; only the universe, the equivalent of self, was to attend. A real spiritual existence was at stake. The duty of the self was to comprehend reality; reality was to be found only in the whole — the universe ; therefore the duty of the individual was to betake himself where the universe in reality was. But the self by its own nature was fitted not only for comprehending the universe, but for being the universe as well; so that to be one's self was the only legitimate aspiration of man. To magnify the self, to have sensations of infinitude, to thrum with the excitement of the universe, was the ambition of the man who went to Walden Pond.

[1] *Journal*, II, 497.

Thoreau speaks in the Journal some thirty times of the excitement which the humming of a telegraph-wire caused within him. " He thought the best of music was in single strains," said Emerson; a single strain of music was for him that "finest strain that a human ear can hear." " The laws of Nature break the rules of Art"; the telegraph-wire told him more about himself — brought the universe closer around him — than the noblest symphony. For symphonies, being civilized, presuppose rules and intelligence, while the telegraph-wire — " When we listen to it we are so wise that we need not to know." [1]

The telegraph-wire, which Thoreau does not mention after 1854 (probably because he thought he had exhausted its meaning), had been significant to him because it had seemed intensely spiritual. It had concentrated into a single strain the meaning of the universe, had furnished him at no expense (at no cost of " life ") the entire spiritual stock which it is possible for man to accumulate. If Thoreau lost faith in the telegraph-wire, he never ceased to believe what Emerson had spent his life preaching: that " spirit" is a single fact, that the soul has a single voice, that all spiritual values are indistinguishably blended in one experience — In-

[1] *The Service*, 13.

spiration. Any source of inspiration suffices;
the exaltation is the thing; man should be ready
to be anything, in the ecstasy of being stimu-
lated. Thoreau never lost faith, as Emerson
never did, in this Inspiration, this facile mo-
nopoly of spiritual privileges. When he found
the world unsatisfactory, he scarcely knew why
— and blamed the world. He scarcely suspected
that his intensity was distilling the essence out
of a vacuum, and not out of life.

Such men, complained Pascal, "inspire no-
tions of simple greatness, and that is not the
state of man." Thoreau's spiritual existence was
more than easy; it was hopelessly, fatally easy.
Assure himself as he might that his own will was
the will of the universe, that thought and feeling are indistinguishable, that soul and body are
one, that necessity is sweet, that good and evil
are phantoms easy to dissolve, yet he never succeeded in stepping entirely out of his little private darkness. Perhaps he read George Herbert's
exhortation, in "The Church Porch," to self-
scrutiny : —

> " By all means use sometimes to be alone.
>   Salute thy self, see what thy soul doth wear.
> Dare to look in thy chest, for 't is thine own,
>   And tumble up and down what thou find'st there."

But if he read it, he read it wrong, read it without the "sometimes"; took it literally and ab-

solutely. And so doing, he fell into the error which Bacon describes as proceeding "from too great a reverence, and a kind of adoration of the mind and understanding of man; by means whereof men have withdrawn themselves too much from the contemplation of nature, and the observations of experience, and have tumbled up and down in their own reason and conceits. Upon these intellectualists," Bacon goes on to say, " which are notwithstanding commonly taken for the most sublime and divine philosophers, Heraclitus gave a just censure, saying, *Men sought truth in their own little worlds, and not in the great and common world;* for they disdain to spell, and so by degrees to read in the volume of God's works; and contrariwise by continual meditation and agitation of wit do urge and as it were invocate their own spirits to divine and give oracles unto them, whereby they are deservedly deluded."

Thoreau deluded himself, not because he was introspective, but because he was introspective in a certain mistaken, fruitless way. His speculations and experiences, intellectual, moral, æsthetic, yielded no important results, not because they were private, but because their privacy was their sole end and aim. Plato and Shakespeare were introspective, and learned to know the world in private; but the world they learned to know was large and important, the "great and common world." They studied themselves along with the rest of the world — Plato his opinions with the opinions of other men, Shakespeare his impressions with the impressions of other men ; Thoreau studied himself alone — his opinions and his impressions by themselves. Shakespeare and Plato, like all men who are versed in the arts of comparison or dialectic, studied themselves as members of the universe; Thoreau studied himself as the universe. Shakespeare and Plato sought to learn their bearings in the world; Thoreau lost sight of bearings, and sought to be the world itself. Thoreau deluded himself precisely in proportion as he refused to keep the very delicate balance which it is necessary for a great and good man to keep between his private and his public lives, between his own personality and the whole outside universe of personalities. Thoreau's introspection was sterile in so far as it was a brooding reverie of self-contemplation rather than an effort to measure and correct and check himself by reference to things beyond himself. His counsel of perfection is meaningless to others in so far as it is intended to be realized in a vacuum, apart from contacts or comparisons ; it was useless to him in that it did not permit of friction with other perfections, did not provide for that jostling and settling into place which the seasoned philosophy of life has undergone. It is clear that Thoreau could not see the bearings of his vacuous and expansive effort: "Is it all my fault?" he asked in the Journal.[1] "Have I no heart? Am I incapable of expansion and generosity? I shall accuse myself of everything else sooner." It is clear enough that he was incapable of distinguishing between fruitless and fruitful expansion — the expansion which merely distends the self at the present stage of its ignorance, and the expansion which really enlarges the self by thrusting it out into play with surrounding selves. Stevenson suggests that " the world's heroes have room for all positive qualities, even those which are disreputable, in the capacious theaters of their dispositions. Such can live many lives, while Thoreau can live but one, and that with continual foresight." Thoreau refused pretty consistently to believe that there was any other life besides his own. " You think," he addressed an imaginary critic in the later Journal,[2] " that I am impoverishing myself by withdrawing from men, but in my solitude I have woven for myself a silken web or *chrysalis*, and, nymph-like, shall ere long burst forth a more perfect creature, fitted for a higher society." A very brave hope, but unrealized anywhere in his career, if the Journal is to be believed.

[1] *Journal*, IV, 314.   [2] *Ibid*., IX, 246.

If it is asked what led Thoreau into his error, what led him to believe he could find out all things by and in himself, perhaps Matthew Arnold gives the keenest answer : " The blundering to be found in the world," says Arnold, " comes from some people fancying that some idea is a definite and ascertained thing, like the idea of a triangle, when it is not." The difficulty with Thoreau, as with many a philosopher during the nineteenth century, was that he had hypostatized an abstraction and seen his own reflection in it. During that century, the seedtime of the modern social soul, when the sun withheld its warmth and mankind suffered growing-pains, abstractions seemed blessed beyond all other commodities because they held out most promise of nourishment, of hope for the solution of the secret of life. When nine tenths of life seemed flowing away, men were wont to seek refuge on the island of an abstraction. When mind and heart and soul were being explained away, men doggedly identified themselves with certain functions of their minds and hearts and souls and demanded immunity. " Elsewhere the world may change, but oh ! not here ! " they cried. Hallowing abstractions in the face of doubt, clutching at phenomena of consciousness in the face of science, they preached and lived vehemently all their lives what right reason condemns as inadequate and provincial. " Work," " Art," " Happiness," " Beauty," " Inspiration," " Reality " rode the century relentlessly. Belief was adequate if sincere and passionate. Men lived fully enough if they represented some quality or aspect of human nature to the consistent exclusion of other aspects and qualities; if they were gripped and warped by a concept or stamped in an attitude, and forgot all else. Men of that time are not so much men as faculties — not so much individual human beings as individual forces. Carlyle is a whole universe in miniature, " creaking, groaning, tortuous." Coleridge, says Sir Walter Scott, is " a lump of coal rich with gas, which lies expending itself in puffs and gleams, unless some shrewd body will clap it into a cast-iron box, and compel the compressed element to do itself justice." Byron is an angry, glowing cheek. Keats is an odor hanging heavily close to the earth. Shelley is a mad bird who would fly higher than is possible. Wordsworth is a column of white mist moving among the hills. Ruskin is a swift, fevered river. Emerson is an electric wire snapping and emitting brilliant, cold sparks. Thoreau is a pard-like hunter, moving quietly whither he likes and refusing to be touched.

Thoreau is one of the most deliberate of all hypostatizers. Born into a philosophical school whose ideas were already well formed, younger by ten years than most of its adherents, and with a craftman's mind for visualizing details, it is no wonder that he, most scrupulously of all men in America or Europe, should have assumed to be real, and attempted to live, the generalizations of Goethe and the abstractions of the transcendental philosophy. Nor is it surprising that, with his passion for the specific, he should have hypostatized a little more strenuously than he did such abstractions as Character, Will, Spirit, Moral Nature of Man, Life, Self, the Present, — that he should have hypostatized more strenuously than he did those abstractions, the quality of " Reality." It is not surprising that a man so quixotically practical should have asserted, when he heard his contemporaries complaining that life had lost its realities, that Reality did exist, and that he would go out and capture it. The hypostatizing of Reality is the simplest of everyday occurrences. Children believe that grown-ups are realler than themselves, and countrymen fancy that real life is to be had for the seeking in cities. The man who went out wolfishly to " live deep and suck out all the marrow of life, to cut a broad swath and shave close, to drive life into a corner, and reduce it to its lowest terms, and, if it proved to be mean, why, then to get the whole and genuine meanness of

it, and publish its meanness to the world," leaves
no one doubting that the monster which pursued
him was Reality hypostatized into life and turned
loose upon him. Reality and its pard-like hunter
— these make up "the Thoreau." Thoreau's
whole life was a search for embodied Reality,
and his whole contention on paper is that Reality is accessible. "How to live, how to get the
most out of life, how to extract the honey from
the flower of the world. That is my every-day
business. I am as busy as a bee about it," is not
the only passage of its kind in the Journal. "Be
it life or death," he adds, "we crave only reality." He is confident that "there is a solid bottom everywhere" if we only have the courage to
sink to it. "Let us settle ourselves and work and
wedge our feet downward through the mud and
slush of opinion and prejudice and tradition,
and delusion, and appearance, . . . to a hard bottom and rock in place — which we can call reality."

When Thoreau says he is seeking "what
was always and always must be because it really
is now," the temptation is irresistible to speculate
upon the probability of his success. It is easy to
guess that he will look nowhere outside himself
for "what really is now." If he finds his self,
he finds reality. If he finds reality, he has found
the universe. "It is only he," said Confucius,

" in the world, who possesses absolute truth who can get to the bottom of the law of his being. He who is able to get to the bottom of the law of his being will be able to get to the bottom of the law of being of other men. He who is able to get to the bottom of the law of being of men will be able to get to the bottom of the laws of physical nature. He who is able to get to the bottom of the laws of physical nature will be able to influence the forces of creation of the Universe. He who can influence the forces of creation of the Universe is one with the Powers of the Universe." Thoreau never gets to the bottom of the law of his being because he fails to keep the other men in mind, because he loses his bearings, because he does not recognize his individual being as in any way distinguishable from universal being. He probes for the bottom of his being in Walden Pond, before he has taken the trouble to be anything among other beings away from Walden Pond. He hopes to find what his self is like absolutely apart from relationships. He hypostatizes " self," sees nothing else, loses its bearings, and so loses it. Like the secret of harmony, it " always retreats as I advance "; and all he can do is to follow helplessly — a nothing in search of a something; a nothing perpetually dividing itself into a something and getting infinity. The problem

of self, like the problem of love, is his sore affliction. "There is no remedy for love but to love
more," said he. So with being; there is no
remedy for being but to be infinitely more — of
nothing.

But it is as much of a mistake, on the whole,
for Thoreau's critic to take him literally, as it
was for Thoreau to take himself so seriously;
few other persons besides the critic are going to
do it. Thoreau's example in society need not be
worried about. The instinct of self-preservation
in humanity and the common capacity for humor
bring it about, of course, that "Walden" is in
general not taken literally. It is easy enough to
point out that Thoreau's main effort came to
nothing; but the likelihood remains that Thoreau
will always count for something among sophisti-
cated persons who take him with the sufficient
allowance of salt. That something, though it be
only a by-product, and though it represent only a
fraction of the man — "I speak out of the best
part of myself," said Thoreau in another connec-
tion — is permanent, and of the first importance.

The best there is in Thoreau is not the naturalist part of him. Emerson predicted that the
example of his usefulness would lead to the creation of a "profession" of naturalist: "I think
we must have one day a naturalist in each village
as invariably as a lawyer or doctor . . . all

questions answered for stipulated fees." But Thoreau the philosopher of human relationships, talking of friendship and charity and solitude, will be remembered when Thoreau the visitor of wild flowers will beg for notice.

Philosophically considered, the best of Thoreau is not his extreme transcendental gospel, the darkest corner of his little private darkness; is not his urging of the elementary; is not his association with a very provincial school which did not know enough in general. If read as scripture, as some of his friends read him, or as madman, as Lowell read him, he will yield nothing. He cannot be taken literally any more than a wild odor can be seized and kept. "I am permitted to be rash," he said in the "Week." It is his temper which is needed and felt, and not his vagaries that need be worshiped or excused. He is a good hater and refuser, and the world likes that now and then. Men like to be pricked; men demand to be made mad on occasions. Men like Thoreau's temper in the atmosphere as much as they like the flavor of his wild apples in their memories. "These apples," he says, "have hung in the wind and frost and rain until they have absorbed the qualities of the weather or season, and thus are highly *seasoned*, and they *pierce* and *sting* and *permeate* us with their spirit"; if his philosophical offering misses richness, it is highly

enough spiced. His sting is far from venom-
ous; " I would give up most other things to be
so good a man as Thoreau," wrote Stevenson to
one of the biographers. No philosophical attack
on Thoreau's individualism can take the tonic
out of his pages or the temper out of his independence. It can be shown that he was unreasonable, and hypostatized " self "; but in " Walden "
(if not in the Journal) he still stands alone,
halfway enviable in his loneliness. Whittier
thought " Walden " " very wicked and heathen-
ish "— but " capital reading." The " Good heart,
weak head " of Emerson furnishes a perpetual
text for Thoreau. The steadfast air of the pages
on philanthrophy in " Walden " should alone
preserve Thoreau's name. An extreme example of self-satisfaction can do no harm in the
twentieth or any century. If Thoreau seems " all
improved and sharpened to a point," his example
nevertheless remains delicious. As long as individual excellence is prized by however slight a
minority, his books will be instructive, says Lowell, " as showing how considerable a crop may be
raised on a comparatively narrow range of mind,
and how much a man may make of his life if he will
assiduously follow it, though perhaps never really
finding it at last."

Thoreau will be found a very satisfactory
spokesman for one who feels driven into a posi-

tion somewhat analogous to his position in 1840.
Not only is he a wholesome shocking force in the
lives of young people who have been brought up
too exclusively on positivistic or humanitarian
principles; he stands pretty staunchly back of
one when one desires to strike at the confident
and benevolent leveler, with his wash of sociality
and sentiment, and when one desires to cry, " I
do not believe you! Man is great!" "Do not
seek so anxiously to be developed," warns Thoreau, " to subject yourself to so many influences,
to be played upon. It is all dissipation." The
greatest apostle of Leisure in his century, he
put to flight Folly's sociological brood, and
only asked for leisure to be good. That his
reaction was unreasonable, and that his refuge
was in an instinct ("immemorial custom" and
"transcendent law") as objectionable as the
socialistic instinct, does not cripple his support
when it is necessary that one be unreasonable. One can be as combative and as asser-
tive now and then as Thoreau was always; one
still "finds it difficult to make a sufficiently
moderate statement"; one still wants to bristle
with indignant hyperbole and paradox in the
humanitarian, scientific, reformatory, or prag-
matic presence. If Thoreau loses in the broadest
sense by being terribly single-minded, he is valuable in a narrower sense by virtue of his very

singleness — valuable as a protestant, valuable as an antidotal flavor.

Thoreau, finally, is an American classic. He will always appeal to the " confirmed city-men " he affected to pity. For the same reason that " Robinson Crusoe " appeals most to land folk, " Walden " will appeal more and more to the men and women of " institutions," to men in studies and clubs, to boys by the fireside in winter. Thoreau is eminently a citizen in the republic of letters, and continues some excellent traditions. " Even his love of Nature seems of the intellectual order," Whitman thought, " — the bookish, library, fireside — rather than smacking of out of doors. . . . I often find myself catching a literary scent off his phrases." The readers of " Walden " will not distrust it because it is literary ; they will treasure it — one cannot say how long — because it is literary, because it is a classic, because it furnishes definite delight. A substantial critic thought " Walden " in 1879 "the only book yet written in America that bears an annual perusal," and remarked that for his own part, with " Walden " in his hands, he could wish " that every other author in America might try the experiment of two years in a shanty." As almost every one has been ambitious to be a second Crusoe, so a few spirits (perhaps more than confess it) will always be furtively suspecting that by two years in the woods they could do themselves some service. "Crusoe" and "Walden," classics of solitude, people do not want to do without.

"No truer American existed than Thoreau," said Emerson. At least no more plain-spoken representative of transcendental New England could be asked for, it seems safe to say. There can be little doubt that the spirit of "Walden" has pervaded the American consciousness, stiffened the American lip, steadied the American nerve, in a ponderable degree. By creating a classic image of the cynic hermit in ideal solitude Thoreau has demonstrated some of the meannesses of the demands of Time and Matter, and furnished the spirit and will for social criticism; he has made men acute critics, if not sensible shepherds, of their own sentiments.

THE END

BIBLIOGRAPHICAL NOTE

BIBLIOGRAPHICAL NOTE

BIBLIOGRAPHIES:

FRANCIS H. ALLEN. *Bibliography of Thoreau.* Boston, 1908. Excellent, and practically complete to 1908.

JOHN P. ANDERSON. Bibliography of Thoreau appended to the *Life* by Henry S. Salt in the Great Writers Series. Briefer, but useful to 1896.

WORKS:

References are to the Walden Edition (with all the "Journal"). 20 vols. Boston, 1906. Almost complete. The other authorized editions are the Riverside Edition, 11 vols., Boston, 1894, and the Riverside Pocket Edition, 11 vols., Boston, 1915. These are without the complete "Journal."

The Service. Ed. F. B. Sanborn. Boston, 1902. The essay does not appear in full under this title in the Walden Edition, although most of the missing parts are to be found in the volumes of the "Journal" in the same edition.

The Bibliophile Society of Boston has privately printed certain fragments of the Journal and other interesting pieces not elsewhere to be found.

BIOGRAPHIES:

W. E. CHANNING. *Thoreau : The Poet-Naturalist.* Boston, 1873, 1902.

H. A. PAGE (A. H. JAPP). *Thoreau, His Life and Aims.* Boston, 1877. London, 1878.

F. B. Sanborn. *Henry D. Thoreau.* American Men of Letters Series. Boston, 1882.

Henry S. Salt. *Life of Henry David Thoreau.* London, 1890. Great Writers Series, 1896.

Mrs. Annie Russell Marble. *Thoreau: His Home, Friends, and Books.* New York, 1902.

Chief Critical Essays:

Emerson, "Biographical Sketch." Prefixed to vol. I of the Walden Edition of Thoreau.

Lowell, "Thoreau." *My Study Windows.*

Stevenson, "Henry David Thoreau: His Character and Opinions." *Familiar Studies of Men and Books.*

Paul Elmer More. *Shelburne Essays.* New York. "A Hermit's Notes on Thoreau," vol. I (1904). "Thoreau's Journal," vol. V (1908).

INDEX

INDEX